THE CINEMA OF LUIS BUÑUEL
by Freddy Buache

$2.95/ £1.05

A lucid and challenging monograph on all Buñuel's films from *Un Chien Andalou* and *L'Age d'or* to *Belle de jour* and *Tristana*.

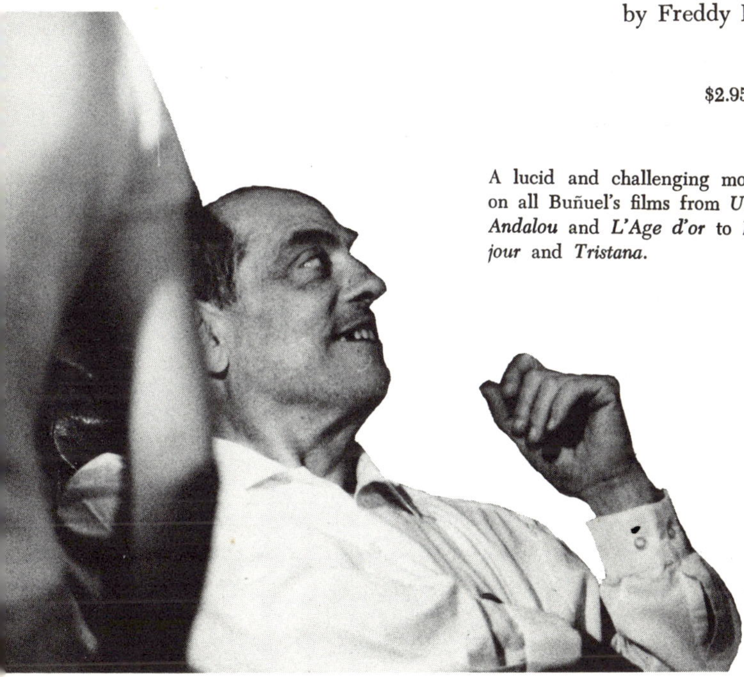

In the same series produced by THE TANTIVY PRESS and edited by Peter Cowie:

EARLY AMERICAN CINEMA by Anthony Slide
GRIFFITH and the Rise of Hollywood by Paul O'Dell
HOLLYWOOD IN THE TWENTIES by David Robinson
HOLLYWOOD IN THE THIRTIES by John Baxter
HOLLYWOOD IN THE FORTIES by C. Higham and J. Greenberg
HOLLYWOOD IN THE FIFTIES by Gordon Gow
HOLLYWOOD IN THE SIXTIES by John Baxter
HOLLYWOOD TODAY by Pat Billings and Allen Eyles
HITCHCOCK'S FILMS by Robin Wood
THE MARX BROTHERS Their World of Comedy by Allen Eyles
FRENCH CINEMA SINCE 1946 (Vol. 1: The Great Tradition)
   (Vol. 2: The Personal Style) by Roy Armes
HORROR IN THE CINEMA by Ivan Butler
THE CINEMA OF JOSEPH LOSEY by James Leahy
SUSPENSE IN THE CINEMA by Gordon Gow
THE CINEMA OF ALAIN RESNAIS by Roy Armes
4 GREAT COMEDIANS Chaplin, Lloyd, Keaton, Langdon by Donald W. McCaffrey
RELIGION IN THE CINEMA by Ivan Butler
THE CINEMA OF FRITZ LANG by Paul M. Jensen
THE CINEMA OF JOHN FRANKENHEIMER by Gerald Pratley
SCIENCE FICTION IN THE CINEMA by John Baxter
THE CINEMA OF ROMAN POLANSKI by Ivan Butler
THE CINEMA OF FRANCOIS TRUFFAUT by Graham Petrie
THE CINEMA OF CARL DREYER by Tom Milne
THE CINEMA OF OTTO PREMINGER by Gerald Pratley
THE CINEMA OF JOSEF VON STERNBERG by John Baxter
THE CINEMA OF JOHN FORD by John Baxter
USTINOV IN FOCUS by Tony Thomas

The Cinema of
LUIS BUÑUEL
Freddy Buache

Translated by Peter Graham

THE INTERNATIONAL FILM GUIDE SERIES
THE TANTIVY PRESS, LONDON
A. S. BARNES & CO., NEW YORK

For Marie-Magdeleine Brumagne and for
Georges Goldfayn

Cover design by Stefan Dreja

English-language edition first published 1973
Original French edition copyright © 1970 by
Editions L'Age d'Homme S.A., Lausanne
English translation copyright © 1973 by The Tantivy Press

Library of Congress Catalogue Card No.: 72-5183
ISBN 0-498-01302-2 (U.S.A.)
SBN 90073048 X (U.K.)

Printed in the United States of America

Contents

	page
UN CHIEN ANDALOU	9
A GOLDEN AGE OF AMOUR FOU	14
THE OTHER SIDE OF THE COIN	30
MORAL AND BIOGRAPHICAL NOTES	37
FROM LONELINESS TO FRIENDSHIP	71
ARCIBALDO DE LA CRUZ	76
THE STYLE	79
ATHEISM	81
LOVE THE REDEEMER	102
EWIE AND HER SHOES	111
VIRIDIANA	117
THE EXTERMINATING ANGEL	127
AFTER THE ANGEL	137
THE DIARY OF A CHAMBERMAID	139
FAITH, DOGMA AND HERESY	151
THE INVISIBLE AND THE VISIBLE	165
Footnotes	186
Filmography	187
Index	206

Stills reproduced by courtesy of La Cinémathèque Suisse, Lausanne, and the author

Octavio Paz has said: "A chained man need only close his eyes, and he will be capable of making the world explode." I would paraphrase his remark as follows: "The screen's white eyelid would only need to be able to reflect the light that is its own, and it would blow up the Universe."

Luis Buñuel

God is dead but the world is encumbered with his corpse.

Georges Bataille

*Buñuel with the author, Freddy Buache,
in Lausanne, during August 1972*

Un Chien Andalou

any artistic work that aims at challenging established values must set out initially to shock, to break clean away from the ubiquitous ethos of family, religion and patriotism.

When Luis Buñuel and Salvador Dali made the short film, *Un Chien Andalou*, in 1929, they deliberately intended to jolt the spectator's peace of mind; and their secondary aim was to put across one of the basic beliefs underlying the whole of surrealist thought: the omnipotence of desire.

This film, which is a kind of openly re-enacted dream, derives from a method known as "paranoia-criticism," which Dali saw as being "based on the critical and systematic objectivisation of delirious associations and interpretations." But the sole aim of the film is not merely to shock, but to have an incendiary effect on people who think they have a clear conscience. When Buñuel published the script in *La Révolution Surréaliste*, he suggested it should be taken as "a desperate, impassioned call for murder." At the same time, he took the opportunity to turn his back firmly on all those art consumers who, either through stupidity, masochism or self-interest, are willing to swallow anything without batting an eyelid, however much it goes against their instincts. Buñuel realised that the only works that could be "retrieved" in this way were those whose charge of spiritual dynamite was easily defused by success. This was why he added the following commentary to his script: "But what can I do about the people who adore all that is new, even when it goes against their deepest convictions, or about the insincere, corrupt press, and the inane herd that saw *beauty or poetry* in something which was basically no more than a desperate, impassioned call for murder?" From then on, Buñuel was to mistrust the superficiality of *stylistic* novelty, which always correlates to fashion (and fashions change

9

so quickly). He preferred to bury his explosives blandly beneath the surface of an apparently traditional style, rather in the same way as Magritte is often able to suggest a quite extraordinary sense of mystery by making almost imperceptible distortions in a painting that is otherwise highly academic.

There is a key image in *Un Chien Andalou:* the eye being cut by a razor blade. But it is not a key that will provide any clear-cut interpretation to this dream-film, which, like all dreams, is both fascinating and disturbing; it simply sets the tone of the film's meandering itinerary. This shock image takes us into a labyrinth whose walls, at once hard and soft, opaque and transparent, either give off a reflection or slide aside—a labyrinth of desire in its various forms. Gradually the constituent elements of the enigma reveal themselves.

Most of the shots have the prosaic, matter-of-fact quality of newsreels. But the film does not restrict itself merely to stating facts: it slowly builds up an hallucinatory feeling of anguish, which is achieved by the unrealistic manner in which realistic images are strung together. There is a flurry of vaguely absurd actions, incongruous objects, and associations of ideas that obey the laws of automatic writing. It would be a mistake to try to work out a systematic exegesis of *Un Chien Andalou,* because it is impossible to translate completely into ordinary language the complexity of this poem—for poem it is, and not a fable or an allegory. On the other hand, it would be equally wrong to see it as the convulsions of two wild imaginations. It *is* open to logical interpretation, and its theme is an extremely serious one. It describes the dramatic collision between desire and the object of that desire in a context that literally bristles with pitfalls. Buñuel and Dali try to show desire as a prisoner that goes round in circles, becomes exasperated, dreams of freedom, goes berserk, fails, springs back to life, veers away from an excruciating state of immobility, and escapes into a dream world. And although I am extremely wary of the sort of pat

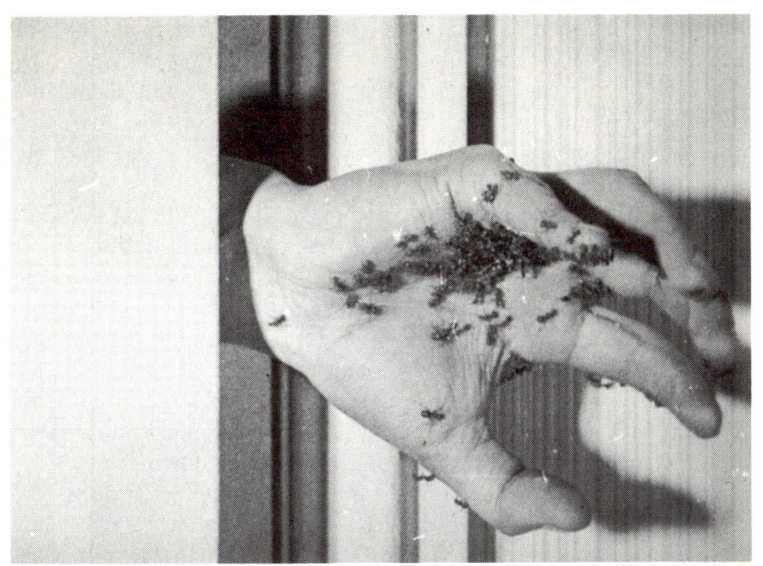

The ant-covered hand in UN CHIEN ANDALOU

interpretation that can be made of the film's transitory propositions, I would nevertheless like to put forward one explanation of it, or at least point towards it. Perhaps I can best begin by quoting part of Jacques Brunius's book, *En Marge du Cinéma Français*—to my mind the only work which, up to now, has dealt with the cinema of that period with any degree of sensibility and insight: "People have tried to discover more inventions in *Un Chien Andalou* than it in fact contains. The Marist monks and rotting donkeys, for instance, that seemed so startling, are again to be found, all over the roads of Spain, in Buñuel's documentary film, *Las Hurdes*. This would seem to contradict Buñuel's own remark that the authors of the scenario systematically steered clear of any image that could be seen as a memory. I suppose it just could be that Buñuel and Dali deliberately thought up the rotting donkeys without ever having seen them, or that Buñuel later used them, in a completely phoney way, for documentary purposes. But one needs only to spend a few minutes in Spain in order to realise that the swarms of cassocks were no invention.

"Many of the elements that go to make up the film are certainly remnants of objective reality, even if the two authors of the scenario were not totally aware of the process. It is the way they are arranged within the film that makes them fit into a mental reconstruction, in exactly the same way as dreams draw on the previous day's experience, and myths are made of scraps of history."[1]

Man is not free to approach the woman he loves. He carries around with him a whole ramshackle load of moral and social circumstances. He is hamstrung, he is weighed down like a slave who has to carry (to use Buñuel's imagery) pumpkins, priests, and a piano laden with rotting donkeys. Nothing could be more grotesquely further from the truth than to say that the pumpkins

The donkey's head (left) and sexual symbolism (right) in UN CHIEN ANDALOU

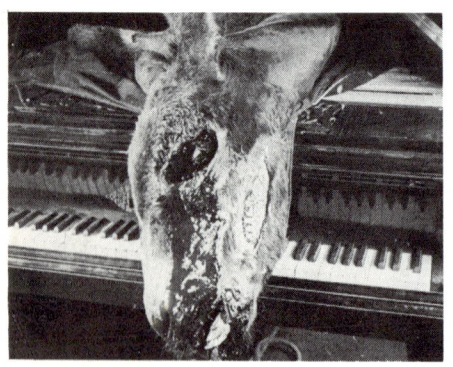
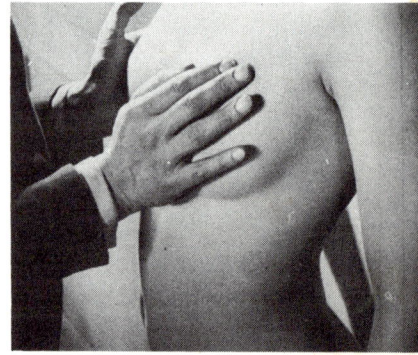

evoke cooking and domestic chores, that the smiling priests represent the way the Church tries to trammel love, that the piano is a symbol of bourgeois life, and that the corpses of animals are reminders of the putrefaction that awaits us from the moment we are born and overtakes us when we die. On the other hand, it does not seem to me to be farfetched to interpret the allusive truth of this sequence as a dynamic symbol that reflects everything which a man must take a grip on if he is to approach the woman he desires. She appears to him as something multiple, as a kind of quarry, an enemy, a beautiful animal with mother-of-pearl flesh, a living statue.

There are countless allusions in the film to suggest that carnal passion is endowed with magical powers. It sweeps away all the constraints normally imposed by time and space, eternalises the moment, brings places closer or takes them farther away, reduces the universe and the passage of years to the unique delights of pleasure granted. *Un Chien Andalou*, through its style, implicitly challenges the conventions of a society that has set a curse on love and has thwarted, gagged (the lover loses his mouth), and racked human desire. It is hardly surprising, therefore, that Jean Vigo was extremely struck by the film's *social* implications as well as its poetic force. On June 14, 1930, when introducing his *A Propos de Nice* at the Théâtre du Vieux-Colombier, Vigo described *Un Chien Andalou* as a "key work and, from the social point of view, accurate and courageous," in the course of his admirable definition of a cinema that dealt at last with "society and its relationship with individuals and things," a cinema that had at last broken away from "the two pairs of lips that take ten thousand feet of film to come together and almost as many to come unstuck again."

But *Un Chien Andalou*, which is marred by a number of gratuitous touches that are probably Dali's doing, remains above all an exploratory, tentative and indirectly aggressive work. In it, the pig-iron is given its preliminary treatment; in *L'Age d'Or* it is enriched and heated until it is white hot. Buñuel's genius is entirely responsible for the latter film (although Dali is credited with collaborating on the script—the only mark he has left on the film is probably, as Ado Kyrou has suggested, the shot of the stroller with a rock on his head). *L'Age d'Or* resorts to the simplest kind of surrealist action—direct insults and a punch in the face.

A Golden Age of Amour Fou

The beginning of *L'Age d'Or*—a brief documentary look at scorpions that is stuck on to the rest of the film in rather the same way as a tram ticket, newspaper cutting or any other mass-produced article is pasted on to a *collage*—sets the whole tone of cool objectivity that follows. The intertitles that occasionally appear during this part of the film take on, as a result, a very particular meaning (one that goes to explain the tremendous power of Buñuel's art): they create an alienation effect whereby the world and our society are subjected to the impassive examination of an experimenter who apparently knows nothing of them. Buñuel first magnifies details for the purposes of analysis, and then reduces the whole to a symbolic synthesis. He clarifies facts in the same way as Eduardo pins butterflies on a board in *Cumbres Borrascosas*. No one has any privileges: the founding of Rome is not given any more importance than the sting of a scorpion, or else, as a corollary, Rome is seen to be just as harmful as a scorpion—and the Vatican is its deadly sting.

These intertitles, then, point actively to this alienation effect. One of them, for instance, which reads: "It [the scorpion] prefers the shade, and provides itself with shelter from the brightness of the sun by crawling under stones," is followed, after several pedestrian informative intertitles of the same kind, by the words: "Sometimes on Sundays . . ." which usher in shorts of quiet streets where the collapse of a building is as commonplace as the blossoming of a rose.

But Buñuel's impassivity is feigned: it conceals a burning passion that transforms itself into a diamond or into phosphorus in order better to scratch or to burn everything it touches. *L'Age d'Or* is the most exhaustive catalogue of oppressions ever compiled for the screen. But it is not just a statistical record that can safely be stowed away in some archive, there to enrich the wizened heritage of western culture. This "pavilion of bloody meat" is a quivering, seething, consuming indictment that calls for rebellion and revolution, while at the same time advocating a liberated, totally unrestricted kind of mad love, or *amour fou*. As André Breton put it: "Never has love, in all that makes it totally restricted to two human beings, isolating them from the outside world, manifested itself in such a free way, or with such cool audacity. Never will the stupidity, hypocrisy and routine of life be able to prevent a work like this seeing the light of day or contradict the fact that on the screen a man and woman inflict the spectacle of an exemplary love on a whole world that is up in arms against them. Such a love contains within it the embryo of a potential golden age (*âge d'or*) that is a complete breakaway from the age of mud which Europe is going through and offers an inexhaustible wealth of *future* possibilities."[2]

We see scorpions coming and going in front of the camera; they attack a rat, or fight each other to the death. The intertitle that follows ("A few hours later . . .") introduces a group of bishops celebrating mass among some rocks: we are immediately plunged into a totally surreal atmosphere that is characterised by the most straightforward realism. In a nearby shack, a collection of broken-down and disabled men in rags (one does not really know whether they are revolutionaries or bandits) are whiling away the time getting together a motley paraphernalia of instruments, which are not only reminiscent of those seen in *Un Chien Andalou* but can be found in all Buñuel's films forming an integral part of the atmosphere: forks, knives, rusty sabres, needles, sticks, rope and string. This pathetic arsenal somehow generates the impression of some ludicrous menace, something which is also suggested by the dialogue: Péman (played by Pierre Prévert) smiles wryly from the pallet on which he is stretched and answers his chief, who is himself pretty feeble-looking and is dressed in the sort of grimy tatters one would expect to see on the poorest farm labourer or stonebreaker, with the following remark: "Yes, I know, but you *do* have accordeons, hippopotami, keys and climbing chiefs . . ." After some more effort, he adds: ". . . and pincers."

Suddenly, an order is given: "The Majorcans have arrived! To arms!" In a small cove at the foot of some cliffs, a flotilla of boats disgorges a crowd of distinguished-looking, self-important people in full evening dress: politicians, ambassadors, ladies from high society, military men, nuns and priests. They quickly form a straggling *cortège* and pick their way across the rugged landscape, leaping from rock to rock, and paying homage, as they go past, to the bishops we saw earlier, who are by now no more than a heap of skeletons and mitres. They prepare to celebrate the laying of the foundation stone of a new city. The most distinguished-looking of them all (who is about as tall as King Victor-Emmanuel and sports a huge moustache) clears his throat before making a speech. He seems to be in some doubts as to whether the pages of his speech are in the right order. Just as he is about to open his mouth, cries are heard: a couple are making love on the muddy track. Uproar ensues. There are shots of a lavatory and of mud, and a huge churning mass of faecal matter invades the screen. The lavatory chain is pulled. The lover (played by Gaston Modot) is arrested. The speaker eventually begins his speech, then takes a trowel and covers the foundation stone with a lump of mortar that looks like a turd. It was on this stone and on this turd, after crushing human love and damning erotic bliss, that imperial Rome,

Modot is arrested in the street in L'AGE D'OR

capital of Christ, was built. A series of documentary shots and a commentary then describe the holy city, and more particularly its traffic problems, thereby showing that the Holy See is always prepared to adapt itself cunningly to changes in customs: "But this very ancient imperial city has also been caught up in the hurly-burly of modern life."

Even so, neither the hatred displayed by the Majorcans nor the despicable Christian authority that unleashes its watchdogs against the happiness of those who are able to love freely manages to separate the lovers. Sexual appetite is stronger than constituted power, its puritan vigilantes, its laws, and its myriad inquisitors and torturers. The handcuffed, frog-marched Modot rebels by kicking a Majorcan dowager's doggie and by squashing a beetle in order to prove (to himself and to others) that he will not give up the struggle. He imagines that the whole world is talking about his lover: he sees her living image on posters and in shop-windows. Love gives him strength. He will flatten anything that comes between him and his desire. He thinks constantly of the woman who awaits him and secretly hopes to meet her again. Meanwhile, in her parents' drawing-room, the last preparations are being made for a society gathering—the beano following the official ceremony—and there is some mundane, simpering chit-chat: "The Majorcans will arrive at nine!" "What about the musicians?" "We have hired four. Six near the microphone will make more noise than sixty of them ten kilometres away."

Modot continues to walk along the street, giving not a thought for anything except the woman he desires, and completely indifferent to the old man who kicks a violin along the pavement towards him, then stamps on it. The woman goes into her bedroom; there is a cow snoozing on her bed. She gently eases it off as though it were a cat. She finds this completely natural because her thoughts are identifying with her desire. And after all, what's wrong, in her stratum of high society, with owning a de luxe cow on top of a couple of pekinese and a poodle? The cow is not only obedient but stylish, and tinkles its bell as it leaves the room. The woman begins to think of her lover. A wind springs up in the room and billows in her hair. Clouds scud across a mirror decorated with daisies. Love refuses to accept space and time: it fills the universe and plunges it into eternity. The sound of the cow-bell gets louder, and is then drowned by the noise of the barking dogs in the park that Modot now finds in front of him: the two desires are seeking, calling and answering each other. The chiming of church bells proves powerless in the face of this sonic harmony. It is at this point that the film reaches its climax of liberating poetry. As

Jacques Brunius said: "*L'Age d'Or*, which is a moral rather than a poetic film, clearly sets out to attack the whole ethos of our civilisation and our society, and in its place advocates a great and forbidden love. What the man must forget is his 'lofty mission' in life, and what the young woman must flout in order to meet him again is the respectability of her family. It is no mere coincidence that we hear music from *Tristan and Isolde*. The blatant irrationality of the film's aggression did not, in any case, escape those who felt they were under fire."[3]

Modot flashes all his credentials in front of his two captors. In a brief flashback, we are told that he is quite a V.I.P. (a delegate of the International Charity Organisation), that the nation places complete trust in him, and that it has decorated him for a fine, upstanding life of self-sacrifice. Needless to say, the policemen release him forthwith. He takes this opportunity to knock into a blind man, then dash off in pursuit of Lya Lys, the lover that so obsesses him.

It is interesting to note how countless, almost imperceptible details all through these sequences combine to create a disturbing atmosphere: characters who bite their lips, hands everywhere, and the woman's bandaged finger that comes across both as an indefinably strange but realistic touch and as a symbol of onanism. Later on, the same sort of disturbing details recur, but in a more emphatic form, rather in the same way as the theme of an overture is first given by this or that instrument, then suddenly developed by the whole orchestra.

The reception is in full swing. The guests pay no attention whatsoever to the various subsidiary incidents that occur: plonque-drinking farmhands drive their cart across the drawing-room, a fire breaks out in the kitchens, and a half-asphyxiated maid rushes out and faints; the game-keeper plays with his small son in the garden, and when the latter plays a practical joke on him he shoots him like a rabbit. This act causes momentary consternation; but in no time the fatuously elegant, respectable, and inane members of this "high society" resume their pleasantries, their hand-kissing, and their polite smiles. Modot arrives on the scene, and sees Lya Lys: their obsessive gaze cuts through the chattering, champagne-drinking assembly. An elderly lady accidentally upsets Modot's glass, and he rewards her with a slap on the face. His behaviour provokes much greater indignation than the murder of the child. Lya Lys slips away into the grounds, and is promptly followed by Modot. The musicians begin to tune their instruments. The two lovers go into a clinch, devour each other with their eyes, kiss, and awkwardly try to identify their two bodies with their two desires. This sublimely poignant and deeply disturbing scene expresses simultaneously the vertiginous limitlessness of erotic transports and the very limitations which are imposed upon them, unbeknown to the two lovers, by their education, their inhibitions and their physical awkwardness that is still further hampered by non-functional clothing and accentuated by some strange need to remain seated in armchairs. They somehow realise that their flesh is incapable of accepting the dazzling challenge of their exaltation. The magic is suddenly nipped in the bud by the intrusion of circumstances from the past and of those inherent in their social and functionary situation. A man-servant appears and says: "Sir, you are wanted on the telephone by the Minister of the Interior." Modot gets up, goes into a study, picks up the receiver and yells: "You scoundrel! Go to hell!" The Minister, choking with emotion, tries to make him change his mind (invoking international tension, riots in the streets, and children to be saved), exclaims that he is totally perplexed and then puts a bullet through his head. Modot goes back to the woman and, through an inner dialogue that again repudiates time and space, they let out the long howl of full orgasm: "My love, my love, my love . . ."

Opposite: six shots from L'AGE D'OR

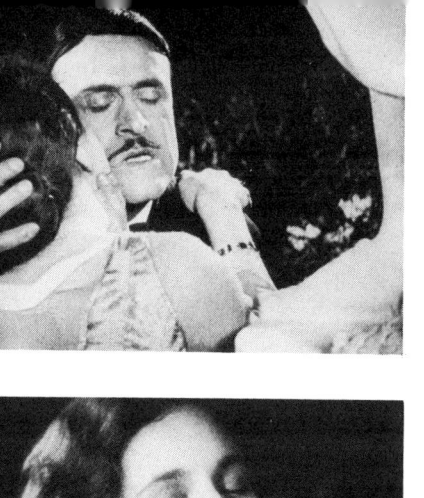

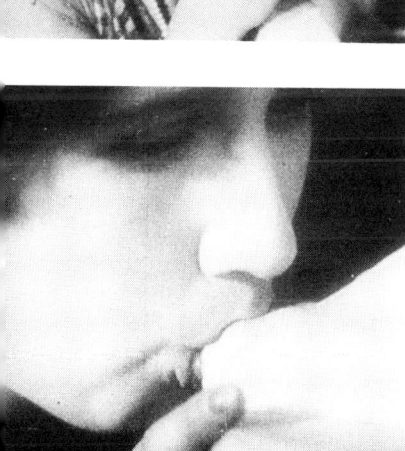
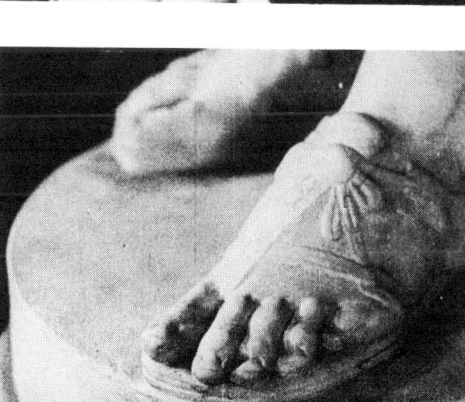

But once again the spell is broken. The bearded conductor of the orchestra (who somehow foreshadows Viridiana's uncle and Tristana's guardian) leaves the pulpit and, mad with jealousy, walks into the garden amid a deafening roll of drums. Lya Lys throws herself into his arms and kisses him on the mouth. Then it is Modot who is swamped by the din of the drums: he goes berserk, bursting pillows, sending clouds of feathers flying, and flinging a motley collection of junk out of a window—various, chaotic signs of his bondage: a plough, a burning tree, a bishop, and a giraffe. As the feathers swirl and the sea beats against the rocks, he gets literally everything out of his system.

The last sequence, a homage to the Marquis de Sade, follows on naturally from this. The survivors of the Château de Selliny (*The 120 Days of Sodom*) stumble out of the castle over the drawbridge after a night of orgy. The Duc de Blangis (who "is, of course, Christ") turns back into the castle, closes its massive door, and brutally murders the sole, bloodstained survivor of their carnage ("a girl of about thirteen"). His beard, which he loses in the process, is next seen fluttering on a huge crucifix in the midst of a blizzard, just as on the soundtrack there starts up a bouncy *paso-doble*.

This summary can do no more than roughly describe this work of quite extraordinary beauty. From beginning to end, the film is intelligently constructed, with a dazzling interplay of editing devices, discrepancies between sound and image, and an extremely concise narrative tissue—in its way it could almost serve as a style manual for the sound cinema. Very important, too, is the humour that permeates several scenes in the curious manner that is one of the hallmarks of Buñuel's genius. The tiniest descriptive touches, which are made without any direct comic or ironic purpose, always derive from the director's wry imagination; he treats them as gags, but instead of making them totally explicit to the point of becoming burlesque, he prefers to show them as a kind of precipitate of

"Flies crawling over the face of a particularly respectable-looking guest" (left) and the Duc de Blangis sans beard (right) from L'AGE D'OR

the absurd, a mischievous reminder of the hidden side of bourgeois conventions (flies crawling over the face of a particularly respectable-looking guest, for instance, or Modot walking out of frame towards the camera, filmed at the level of his somewhat rebellious fly-buttons).

The film's explosive combination of subconscious urges and relentless social criticism did not elude the upholders of order and tradition, although a series of public showings did take place at the Studio 28 cinema without incident. But on December 3, 1930, the Jeunesses Catholiques (a Catholic youth movement), and members of the Ligue des Patriotes and the antisemitic Ligue Antijuive damaged the screen with oxide and ink, tore up the cinema seats, and destroyed the exhibition of surrealist painting that was being held in the foyer. This reaction brought the whole of the right-wing press out against the film, and an urgent question was put by M. Le Provost de Launay, a Paris councillor, to the Préfecture de la Police. The cinema manager, M. Mauclaire, was fined, *L'Age d'Or* was banned on December 11, and all copies seized on the twelfth. Police action did not end there. Censors all over the world deemed the film explosive. In 1935, for instance, Franco, the then governor of the Canaries, banned it and ordered the seizure of the copy that was to be shown during the surrealist exhibition at Santa Cruz de Ténérife. This violent defence reflex on the part of the authorities is proof indeed that Buñuel's film hit the nail on the head; and it still hits just as hard.

No other film has ever deciphered the structures of a society better than *L'Age d'Or*; the society in question is our own, even though it may give the false impression of having evolved since 1930. It still camouflages its criminal hypocrisy behind starched dickeys, uniforms and cassocks, behind slogans about the wisdom of the nations of the world and the twin myths of human nature and original sin, and behind Christian morality in general (as interpreted historically—and most ingeniously—by those in power in a bourgeois, capitalist society). Buñuel demonstrates how love is able to destroy established order, and why it is vital for it to do so if there is to be any hope of founding a form of humanism that is truly the measure of man and is stripped clean of idealistic mumbo-jumbo and fallacious freedom.

The lengthy manifesto brought out by thirteen surrealists just after the *L'Age d'Or* scandal displays a keen understanding of the film's power and relevance. Towards the end of this valuable document, there is the following passage, under the sub-heading "Social aspect—Subversive Elements"[4]:

"One would have to go a long way back into the past in order to find a cataclysm comparable to the age in which we live. One would probably have to go right back to the collapse of the ancient world. It would be nice if the curiosity that incites to take an interest in those times of great upheaval—times that were, relatively speaking, fairly similar to our own—were able to derive something more than mere history from that period. A Christian heaven, alas, has completely obliterated everything else, and there is nothing in it that one has not already seen on the ceilings of the Ministry of the Interior or on rocks by the seaside. This is why the genuine traces left on the human retina by the needle of a great mental seismographer will always be, unless they disappear along with everything else when capitalist society is annihilated, of utmost importance to those whose chief concern is to define the critical point at which reality is replaced by 'simulacra.' Whether the sun sets for good and all depends on the will of mankind. Projected at a time when banks are being blown up, rebellions breaking out and field guns rumbling out of arsenals, *L'Age d'Or* should be seen by all those who are not yet disturbed by the news that censors still let the newspapers print. It is an indispensable moral complement to a stockmarket scare, and its effect will be direct precisely because of its surrealist nature. For there is no fictionalisation of reality. The first stones are laid, conventions become a matter of dogma, the police are as free with their truncheons as they always are, and, as always too, various accidents occur within bourgeois society that are received with total indifference. These accidents, which, it will be noticed, are presented in Buñuel's film as philosophically pure, weaken the powers of endurance of a rotting society that is trying to survive by using the clergy and the police as its only buttresses . . ."

The manifesto ends with a passage that has more relevance than ever since the 1968 May events in France: "In a period of 'prosperity,' the social usefulness of *L'Age d'Or* must be established by the degree to which it satisfies the destructive needs of the oppressed, and maybe also by the way in which it panders to the masochistic tendencies of the oppressors. In spite of all the danger that it may be suppressed, this film will, we feel, serve the very useful purpose of blazing through skies never as beautiful as those it shows us in the mirror [of Lya Lys's dressing table]."

Further to these remarks, I would only add that Buñuel's incessantly subversive action results in a many-sided poetic force that will occasionally lead me to use the word "eroticism" in reference to his work. It must be remembered that in the context of a monograph devoted to this director, the term is not used in at all the same way as it has been for the last few years or so to describe a certain brand of sexy film. In order to preclude any misunderstandings, I had better define my terms.

Eroticism is a strictly subjective idea that consequently varies according to the individual and to the period of civilisation in which he lives. At the same time, eroticism is a value, or, if you like, a means that freedom uses in order to consummate itself. It shows human beings how to use one of their most directly intelligible powers to challenge a moral code whose oppressiveness is always bound up with oppression of a social and political nature.

This type of eroticism, because it calls for the breaking of taboos, lies at the basis of one of the motivations for the war we have to wage against the injustice, hypocrisy and enslavement of our society. To understand it fully, one has to have read Georges Bataille, and remember that he once wrote: "Eroticism cannot be considered independently of the history of labour and of the history of religion." This is the kind of eroticism we find in Buñuel—converted into magnetic waves and not simply into a peepshow for voyeurs. It derives from the *amour fou* as defined by André Breton, and comes close to the sublime love as imagined by Benjamin Péret in an extremely important text called *Le Noyau de la Comète* (The Nucleus of the Comet): "Sublime love implies the most total sexual freedom possible. Without it, the possibilities of choice can only remain ludicrously small. The justification of this freedom is therefore to be found in the aims it enables to be achieved. This is not true today, where sexual freedom remains dissociated from love. Instead of increasing the number of possible choices, it results in the creation of an area of non-choice, which causes fresh hindrances to the triumph of sublime love. The ramparts of sexual prejudice have been cleared, but they camouflaged a hitherto unsuspected quicksand: aimless sexual licence can only debase human beings just like the strictest taboos, instead of uplifting them in the way that sublime love does; but whereas taboos are occasionally capable of setting the human spring, sexual licence can only wear it out, and moreover is likely to usher in a new period of sexual constraint. History is full of examples. Far be it from me to put up the slightest opposition to this newly acquired sexual freedom—after all, the blossoming of sublime love is conceivable only in a society that has been delivered from every kind of shackle. It nevertheless remains that this concession has been granted, by a society that is basically hostile towards love and all genuine freedom, because .it offers absolutely no threat to its structure or ideals, and because it temporarily diverts men's attention from more concrete conquests. True to character, this society has quite naturally dissociated the container from the content in order to keep the mind and the flesh fundamentally separate from, and hostile towards, each other, just as it still persists in setting the heart and reason at variance, in causing men to feel hostility towards each other."[5]

Herbert Marcuse echoes Péret in *Eros and Civilization:* "The self-indulgent display of erotica in magazines, cinemas and advertisements is but one of the attractive disguises used by a civilisation in frantic pursuit of happiness in order to mystify the masses a little more efficiently. In an almost Pavlovian manner, the consumer is fed stereotypes: men are shown women with figures as slinky as E-type Jaguars, and women are allured with the manliness of a James Bond or a managing director at cocktail time. Cigarette or airline advertisements proffer images of an ideal couple off for a weekend or a cruise, in true Playboy style, with coitus as part of the package. The escalation of this kind of visual audacity results in the futile reprobation of Mrs. Mary Whitehouse & Co., and acts as a most useful safety-valve for the moral status-quo:

there is no threat to general happiness, and the era of profit-making can go on existing because women are still objects and men work their fingers to the bone in order to earn money just in order to be able to spend it, and because, as Simone de Beauvoir put it, they are happy with "pretty pictures." Contrary to what optimists think, there is absolutely no getting rid of taboos; they are replaced by other taboos, or else camouflaged. True, it may well be that it is no longer a Christian God that is hindering genuine sexual freedom, but the God of increment and his prophets, the businessmen; economic considerations take cover behind biblical ones so as to disguise their more blatant characteristics, whereas in the past the opposite was true. Now original sin consists of not having a bank account or of not being able to keep up with the Joneses. Relations between men and women are now guided by considerations of status, which have supplanted the former concepts of character and fortune or of breeding. Moreover, every day people's bodies are increasingly treated as objects, square pegs to be fitted in the round moulds of top models (whether masculine or feminine), and the ephemeral contact of two epidermes has now taken on an outdoor, hygienic character that is totally devoid of any passion. Biological pasteurisation has taken over from the theological pasteurisation of carnal love. There is no danger in giving such robots the illusion that they are free to cause sparks: if they are properly programmed (and our computer experts will see to that!), their icy sparks will never cause a conflagration.

To get back to *L'Age d'Or*, although Dali is, as I have mentioned, credited with having worked on the film, the two men could not be less alike.

Buñuel could not be less interested in the dollars that are for the taking if one is a blustering opportunist, or in the sort of notoriety that newspaper columnists devote to murderers, sports, champions, exhibitionist artists and con-men in general. So it is not surprising that when he talked of *L'Age d'Or*, in an interview with

Manuel Michel in 1965,[13] he adopted a modesty of tone that may have disguised the pertinence of his remarks:

— But do you no longer believe then that ideological scandal can be a useful form of intellectual terrorism?

— As I have already said, it was useful in the past. If you remember, I quoted what Breton said to me: "My dear friend, nowadays it's no longer possible to scandalise anyone." And he was right. How is it possible to shock after the Nazi mass murders and the atom bombs dropped on Japan? I feel that today the use of scandal is a negative action. *L'Age d'Or*, which in its day was a militant film that aimed at raping clear consciences—and was therefore scandalous—is now a harmless work that was applauded by the audience at the Lincoln Center in New York when it was shown there recently. And when the film was shown in London for twelve consecutive days, no one got up and protested: there was just one old lady who wrote to say that she found the film "shocking."

— But to judge by the films you've made, it would not seem that you have abandoned your principles.

— My principles, no. But I do think one has to modify one's method of attack, although one's aims remain essentially the same—for the moral oppression has remained unchanged, it has simply assumed another disguise. What I am aiming to do in my films is to disturb people and destroy the rules of a kind of conformism that wants everyone to think that they are living in the best of all possible worlds.[6]

The Other Side of the Coin

There is not the slightest trace of a hiatus between *L'Age d'Or* and *Las Hurdes*. Buñuel unceremoniously plunges us "into the icy waters of selfish motivations." This fragment of one of Marx's sentences, from the opening pages of the *Communist Manifesto*, was at one point considered by Buñuel as one of the possible variants (along with *La Bête Andalouse*) of the title of *L'Age d'Or*, and Breton, in *L'Amour Fou*, deplores the fact that an expurgated version of the film, with that "childishly reassuring" label, was shown in workers' cinemas. It is true that the role of *L'Age d'Or* cannot be reduced to that of an inflammatory tract in the service of a single party against the bourgeoisie, because it is a film that concerns both the totality of each individual and the totality of all individuals. In this connection, Breton wrote: "Every time a man loves, nothing can prevent him from involving the sensibility of all mankind in his act."

Las Hurdes, an "essay in human geography," shot from April 20 to May 24, 1932, describes an area of Spain and its inhabitants with all the objective realism of a scientist, and the documentary horror of the subject matter makes the film at once a nightmare and a piece of social criticism.

The mountainous region of Hurdes is situated less than one hundred kilometres south-west of Salamanca, between Sierra de la Peña de Francia and Sierra de Gata. At the time the film was shot, a population of ten thousand people were mouldering away in fifty or so tiny villages.

Twenty kilometres before entering Hurdes country, which is not linked by road to the outside world, Buñuel lingers a moment at the last village, La Alberca. It is a day of festivity. A wedding has just taken place, and the inhabitants perform a strange and barbarous rite; men on horseback ride at full tilt at a cock that is hanging by its feet from a rope stretched across the street and try to tear off its head. Then the cock's head is triumphantly carried throughout the village, while the inhabitants drink themselves into a stupor: a cruel preamble to discovery of the Hurdanos. Then the camera takes us into rugged, desolate country, where Christianity was introduced by the Carmelites. The ruins of their monasteries overlook crouching, windowless, chimneyless dwellings with roofs of flat stones, where men, women and children huddle in horrifying conditions of physical and mental hygiene. The commentary adds: "In the Hurdes, we never heard anybody sing."

The families all live in a single room. The water from a stream is used for everything. And yet here, as everywhere, the sum of the angles of a triangle is equal to two right angles, and the moral education received by the school children is the same as elsewhere. A little boy writes "respect your neighbour's property" on the blackboard in a schoolroom where on one of the walls an engraving has been pinned which shows a bewigged and powdered noblewoman dressed in Eighteenth century clothes—a dramatic confrontation of the two faces of the same class-ridden society. By making visually explicit the relationship between concrete suffering and the abstract universality of an engraving, the film instantly juxtaposes, in a highly revealing situation, the contradictions that are eating away our society. In a flash, it destroys the inevitability of injustice: it is no longer possible to find a reason for it in theological explanations.

Injustice is the product of a human order which through the clever use of parables about Good and Evil makes a travesty of the most basic notions of justice. Buñuel tears away the mask and points an accusing finger at the syphilitic faces and running sores that form part of a world crucified by Christianity—a religion that always sends priests to accompany oppressors so that they can bless the victims and clear the consciences of the criminal defenders of property, tradition and order (this is of course an attitude that is deplored by clearsighted Christians, and is certainly one of

LAS HURDES

the main reasons for the crisis that has been shaking the Roman church since the middle of the Twentieth century).

The decomposition of the collectivity of Hurdanos takes its course with a terrifying, blind logic that leaves no room for hope. This irreversible movement of life towards its own negation becomes unbearably cruel when seen through the prism of the art that is expressing it: there are shots where the realism is intentionally given a touch of the tragic, romantic and melodious music on the soundtrack, and a commentary terser than a chemistry lecture. This aesthetic approach lends the whole reportage an air of fantasy: because the land is too dry, the Hurdanos do not raise farm animals; only those who are slightly less poor manage to feed a pig; but they do not keep it very long. As soon as there is a bit of flesh on it, they kill it and eat it over three days. The bee-hives to be seen in that part of the country do not belong to the Hurdanos; their owners in La Alberca get them brought down to town on donkeys; sometimes a donkey kicks against the pricks and falls, crushing the hive and causing the bees to sting it to death. Its flesh is then torn to pieces by a stray dog. May is the toughest month for the Hurdanos; the only thing they have to eat are cherries, but as they cannot wait they eat them while still unripe and give themselves dysentery. They laboriously collect earth, sometimes very far away up in the mountains, and deposit it in sackfuls in walled plots by the riverside; but these paltry kitchen gardens are not very productive as their artificial soil soon loses its fertility —the lack of farm animals means no manure. This is why it is in their interest that their own beds should produce good fertiliser; so they sleep fully dressed on leaves that ferment to make a compost. When one of them is bitten by a viper, the bite is very often not fatal, but because they try to heal the wound with herbs they infect it and the victim dies. Intermarriage encourages the degeneration of the Hurdanos, who are already old men by the age of thirty. There is no lack of cripples, dwarves and idiots. They are all afflicted with malaria. Death is the only event that breaks the awful monotony of their countless woes. The family carries the corpse for miles over the hills to a weed-covered cemetery. At night, an old madwoman rings a bell and intones prayers as she shuffles through the streets. It is quite literally the auctioning of death. She says: "Nothing keeps one more on the alert than the constant thought of death. Recite an *Ave Maria* so that so-and-so's soul may rest in peace."

Before evoking this continual presence of death in the region of Las Hurdes at the end of the film, the commentary alludes to an incidental fact: "The only luxurious things we came across in Las Hurdes were the churches . . ."

This list of facts becomes increasingly spell-binding because of the way in which it identifies reality with nightmare and is at the same time both accurate and hard-hitting; in the middle of it Buñuel suddenly inserts a didactic sequence about the anopheles mosquito (with diagrams to boot). This of course is no mere digression, nor is it a mere flourish stuck into the film in order to stimulate a page or two of waffle about *collage* by the vaguely structuro-marxist critics of the Parisian smart set. On the contrary, this seemingly irrelevant sequence plays exactly the same role as the remarks about scorpions, the shots of Rome, and some of the intertitles in *L'Age d'Or*. This device, which is reminiscent of Max Ernst's method of fixing a T-square or some similar object on to a painting, prevents the narrative from lapsing into poetic ghoulishness: this brief sequence, as well as the host of objective and informative details to be found throughout the film, gives the nightmare just the right dose of reality and forces the spectator to look for the basic causes, nipping in the bud any urge he may feel to pity the Hurdanos. For pity—and this is one of the main themes underlying *L'Age d'Or*—is the sister of resignation and the very basis of moral dishonesty; it provides every individual who is too cowardly to engage in revolt with a weighty, yet specious alibi.

By getting across the alienation of the Hurdanos without a trace of pathos, Buñuel is in fact postulating that there is but one last hope for them. There is something of all of us in these Hurdanos, victims of themselves and of others. As we, who are chronically overfed, watch these Beckettian creatures in the strangulating syndrome of extreme poverty, we somehow realise that we are their brothers because our human universe, like theirs, is one of scarcity—but on another level. Polluted air and chemically contaminated food are our unripe cherries. What we most lack is time to live.

If Buñuel decided to return to his country in the spring of 1932 to shoot *Las Hurdes*, it was probably because the political situation seemed very promising. After the elections of April 12, 1931, King Alphonso XIII decided to go into exile. At the end of the year, the Constitution of the Second Republic was passed by the Cortes. It planned the enforcement of several anticlerical acts aimed at radically transforming state education, the relations between State and Church, and the power of religious bodies. These decisions, even before they were enforced, ran into fierce opposition. In May 1931, Cardinal Segura, Archbishop of Toledo and primate of Spain, in a pastoral letter that caused a considerable stir, asked his flock to fight "those who want to destroy religion." After his pronouncement, the various enemies of the Republic united in a common front. Monarchists, army officers and aristocrats took provocative action in Madrid on May 10, 1931. The people responded by setting fire to cars in the streets and to the offices of the conservative

The village in LAS HURDES

newspaper *ABC*. The army stepped in, causing violent counter-demonstrations the following day. In Calle de la Flor, in the heart of the capital, the Jesuit Church was burnt down, as well as several other churches and convents.

Within a few days, similar arson was committed elsewhere, even in outlying provinces. The new War Minister, Manuel Azaña, declared that he preferred to see all the churches of Spain burnt down rather than allow the hair of a single republican to be touched. At that time, there were some million and a half anarchists in Spain who formed part of the large union organisation CNT (Confederacion Nacional del Trabajo). Under the influence of their quite remarkable leaders, the anarchists reacted strongly to the action of the monarchists. They called a number of impressive strikes during the summer. Two people were killed in San Sebastian, and thirty (with two hundred wounded) in Seville. In spite of a government ban, a CNT meeting was held in Estramadure, a small village in Castilblanco, resulting in the intervention of the Guardia Civil; four members of the latter were killed, and their bodies savagely mutilated. Similar incidents occurred all over Spain.

The anticlerical legislation was complemented by agrarian reform which was also a direct threat to the church, as it owned two-thirds of all land. The government was attacked in an increasingly virulent fashion by right-wing elements. But as it baulked at taking its action as far as was demanded by the leaders of the CNT (where there was a very strong delegation of small farmers and farm workers), it was also attacked by the Left. When Alcala Zamora, a Catholic, was designated President of the Republic, he failed to reconcile the various elements of a nation that was racked by countless conflicts.

It was against this background of crisis that Buñuel, who had taken up an intransigent Republican stand, made *Las Hurdes*. His masterpiece was originally a film specifically intended to help a militant cause. It was, in the end, banned by an indecisive government that was caught between two fires.

Moral and Biographical Notes

Luis Buñuel Portolès was born on February 22, 1900, in the middle of the sierra of Teruel (Aragon). His father, Leonardo Buñuel, who was born in 1852, left his family at the age of fourteen and joined the army. He took part in the Cuban-American war, and settled down in America where he started a hardware business. He returned to his native country in 1899 and married the very beautiful Maria Portolès, who was thirty years his junior. Born in 1882 (she died in 1969), she gave him seven children: Luis, the eldest, Maria (1901), Alicia (1902), Conchita (1904), Leonardo (1907), who became a doctor, Margarita (1912), and Alfonso (1915), an architect who became a member of the Spanish Surrealist group.

Luis always displayed great devotion and admiration for his mother. Though his family owned land in Calanda, they lived in Saragossa, where Luis grew up and was educated. But during his childhood he returned regularly to Calanda for the summer holidays, Christmas and so on. And although when he was an adolescent he usually spent his holidays in San Sebastian, he never missed staying in his native village, at least during Holy Week. As a result, Buñuel, who was born of a wealthy, bourgeois landowning family, was equally well acquainted with town and country life. A clear idea of his early days can be gained from the memoirs of his sister, Conchita,[7] a number of interviews, and the remarkable work of J. Francisco Aranda.[8] Conchita, for instance, writes: "Luis got top marks at school quite effortlessly, out of innate intelligence. It got to a point where shortly before the end of the school year he deliberately committed a terrible misdemeanour in order to avoid the humiliation of being top dog at prize-giving day. We were fascinated by his boarding school life, and gleaned our information during the family evening meal. Once, Luis told us that at the school lunch he had found a filthy pair of Jesuit's black underpants in his soup. My father, who made a principle of sticking up for the school and its teachers on all occasions, refused to believe him. When Luis declined to change his story, he was sent out of the dining room; he walked out with great dignity, paraphrasing Galileo: "Even so, there *was* a pair of underpants." Later on, she says, "Luis began to talk to the family about his desire to become an agricultural expert. The idea went down well with my father, who could already see him making improvements in our estates in lower Aragon. But my mother was horrified: it was a career that could not possibly be prepared for in Saragossa. But this was precisely what appealed to Luis: in order to study he would have to leave Saragossa and his family. He took his degree quite brilliantly." Elsewhere, she says: "When he was about thirteen, Luis began to learn the violin. He was very keen on the instrument, partly because he seemed to be gifted for it. He waited until we were in bed, then, violin in hand, he would walk into the bedroom where I and two sisters of mine used to sleep; he used to begin by playing the 'subject,' which I realise now, as I look back, must have been very Wagnerian even though at the time he wasn't any more aware of this than we were. At that period, we used to spend each summer at our house in Calanda. Luis managed to form an orchestra, and during extremely solemn religious ceremonies, he would play phrases from Perosi's *Mass* or Schubert's *Ave Maria*, to the great delight of the congregation."

When one learns as well that this mischievous and resilient boy, who certainly had no aversion for physical pursuits (he later went in for boxing), was also an imaginative child who loved to play with a little theatre and cardboard characters, one realises that his

Truffaut, Buñuel, Jeanne Moreau, and Albert Finney receiving awards in Rio, 1962

mind was a balanced mixture of dream and ludic invention. He loved nature, but because of his scholastic gifts he had very keen intellectual tendencies. He wanted to devote his time to the observation of animals (he always kept one or two in his room—a rat, a snake, an owl, or some beetles). More particularly he was keen to study biology or, better even, entomology; but at the same time he wondered whether music might not be his true vocation. He was a tireless reader of the Scriptures, and was able to recite long passages of it by heart.

While highly conscious of his cosy family life and open to mystical exaltation, he nevertheless felt the need to break away. He became increasingly aware that his strict Catholic education was stifling both his physical and moral vitality. He later admitted that his adolescence was dominated by two feelings: a profound erotic urge that was at first sublimated by strong religious beliefs, and a deep-rooted consciousness of death.

After attending the Jesuit College founded in Saragossa by friars who had been expelled from France, he moved to Madrid at the age of seventeen. He took up lodgings in the "Residencia de Estudiantes," and made friends with Roman Gomez de la Serna, José Ortega y Gasset, Guillen, Alberti, Altolaguirre, Salvador Dali, José Bergamin and above all Federico Garcia Lorca. All the creative talent which emerged from the "Residencia" and which made the so-called generation of '25 so famous was itself nurtured by teachers of the equally famous generation of '98. It was in this seething cultural atmosphere that Buñuel became interested in literature and drama, read Freud's *Psychopathology of Everyday Life,* and discovered the cinema. He wrote film reviews and founded a university film society. In this way, he thoroughly familiarised himself with the medium, and when he went to Paris he had no difficulty in moving into the circle of the men who shared his preoccupations, the Surrealists.

No more need be said of *Un Chien Andalou, L'Age d'Or,* and *Las Hurdes* (except that they were all made outside the conventional commercial system, with money provided by his mother, the patronage of the Vicomte de Noailles, and the lottery winnings of a friend called Acin). It seemed for a time that after this volcanic eruption on to the film scene Buñuel had chosen to go into the wilderness, just as Rimbaud disappeared into the depths of Abyssinia.

After making *Las Hurdes,* he did some dubbing work in France, became a producer in Madrid, and then offered his services to the Republican Government, which sent him on a special mission to Hollywood.

In the interview Buñuel gave to André Bazin and Jacques Doniol-Valcroze,[9] he talked about this period in his life: "After *Las Hurdes,* I worked in Paris. I no longer wanted to make films. Thanks to my family, I had enough to live on, but I was rather ashamed of not doing anything. So I worked for two years with Paramount in Paris, doing dubbing, and then was sent to Spain by Warner Bros. to supervise their co-productions. I also did some more dubbing there. Then I began to produce some films in collaboration with a friend of mine, Ricardo Urgoiti. There were four of them; they were of no interest at all, and I can't even remember their titles. Then the Spanish Civil War broke out. I thought this was the end of the world, and that I ought to find something better to do than making films; I offered my services to the Republican Government in Paris. They sent me to Hollywood in 1938 on a "diplomatic mission" to supervise, as technical adviser, two films that were to be made about the Spanish Republic. Then suddenly the war was over, and there I was, stuck in America without friends or a job. Thanks to Miss Iris Barry, I found employment at the Museum of Modern Art. I thought we were going to do great things, but in the end it turned out to be a bureaucratic job. I had fifteen or twenty people under me. I was in charge of Spanish versions for Latin America. I stuck it out for four years. In 1942 I was forced to hand in my resignation because I was the director of *L'Age d'Or*. Miss Iris Barry accepted my resignation with tears in her eyes. It was the day that the news of Mers-el-Kébir came through, and there was a really dramatic atmosphere. I refused to give an interview to the journalists who came to see me—I felt that at such a time it wasn't really all that important whether Mr. Buñuel was or was not working for the Museum. I was depressed; I had no savings, and I spent the next few weeks as best I could, in fact pretty awfully. And then the American Engineering Corps took me on as a commentator for Spanish versions of films made by the American Army. In twenty or so films my 'fine voice' could be heard expatiating on welding methods, explosives and aeroplane parts."

Then Buñuel went from New York to Hollywood, where Warner

Bros. offered him a similar job. He spent two years there. As he was well paid, he was able to save up enough money to stop working for a year. By 1946 he had run through his savings, and moved to Mexico. There he met Denise Tual, with whom he planned to shoot an adaptation of Lorca's *La Casa de Bernarda Alba* in France. He also met the producer Oscar Dancigers and made a film for him that was a piece of straight commercial entertainment. According to Buñuel,[10] "there was a lot of singing in it, tangos and whatnot. It was called *Gran Casino*. The story was set in Tampico at the time when they were drilling for oil. The scenario wasn't bad at all, but the film starred the two best-known Mexican and Argentine singers, Jorge Negrete and Libertad Lamarque. So I had them singing all the way through—it was like a championship match between them. The film didn't do very well, and I spent two years out of work. In the end, Dancigers did ask me to put up an idea for a children's film. I gingerly suggested the scenario of *Los Olvidados,* which I had written with my friend Luis Alcoriza. He liked it, and told me to work on it. Meanwhile, he found he had a chance to produce a commercial comedy; he suggested I shoot that first, and in exchange he would give me considerable artistic freedom on *Los Olvidados*. So I shot *El Gran Calavera* in sixteen days, and it was a great success. Then I was able to get down to *Los Olvidados*. . . ."

El Gran Calavera is a pleasant piece of froth that follows all the canons of the commercial Mexican cinema. Buñuel gave only halfhearted attention to the making of it, and is right in dismissing it as one of his very minor works. There are, however, one or two situations that take a surprising turn; and the *clichés* of music hall and melodrama are sometimes turned inside out by twists in the plot. A roisterer who has been shut up in a cell with a lot of scruffy jailbirds is politely requested to come out. We realise immediately that the man is of a different social class from his unfortunate co-detainees. In fact, he is a millionaire who has been drowning his sorrows in drink ever since the death of his wife. And Don Ramiro has also been neglecting his business affairs. His family is furious at the idea of his riches being frittered away on a life of debauchery, and tries to take advantage of the situation by getting hold of the money and spending it on more worthwhile things than drink. They make him believe he is ruined, move to a poor district, and all knuckle down to work in exemplary fashion in the hope that this will bring the playboy back to his bourgeois senses. But the rescue operation fails: Don Ramiro tries to commit suicide. In the course of his failure to do away with himself, he cottons on to the plot and with malicious relish decides to turn the idea to his own advantage. With the help of evidence faked by him, the members of his family learn that he is bankrupt. Convinced as they are that the work they imposed upon themselves out of venality will now be absolutely essential if they are to keep up their style of living, they derive a certain happiness from it. A love element intervenes. A worker called Pablo falls in love with Don Ramiro's daughter, Virginia. To earn a little extra money on top of his ordinary wages, Pablo drives round the city in an old car fitted out with two loudspeakers that enable him to blare out advertising slogans. One day, he takes Virginia with him on his rounds and tells her how much he loves her, but forgets to switch off the mike! This broadcasting in the streets of his declaration of love—a funny, moving expression of *amour fou*—is not enough to make Virginia, who has been brought up in a petit bourgeois milieu that frowns on reckless extravagance, rebuff the attention of a cretinous money-bags: she even agrees to marry him. At the very last moment, her father calls off the wedding in order to prevent love being crushed by money.

After this trial run, Buñuel was finally able to start working on something he felt really deeply about, *Los Olvidados;* this film, which was shown at the 1951 Cannes Film Festival, marked Buñuel's triumphant come-back. From that moment on, he treated Mex-

The threat of violence in LOS OLVIDADOS

ico, the land of his exile, as his native country, and his creative career again began to bear fruit.

Very often he was unable to find a producer for his own subjects, and had to fall back on directing adaptations of novels he had not himself chosen to film. But he was always inventive enough to manage to give these subjects his own characteristic non-conformist slant. I remember, for instance, the furious reaction of a businessman, who said to me: "We asked Buñuel for an adaptation of John Knittel's *Thérèse Etienne*. Well, my friend, what he came up with had nothing to do with *Thérèse Etienne*: it was pure Buñuel!" It would be hard to find a neater, more straightforward way both of paying homage to a genuine creator and of damning the fathom-

The urchins in LOS OLVIDADOS

less fatuity of businessmen whose merchandise happens to be exposed film (Buñuel's project for *Thérèse Etienne*, although well advanced, then of course ground to a halt, and the producers handed over the subject to a run-of-the-mill French director with a double-barrelled name who turned out a terrible piece of work that was a deserved box-office flop).

Like many other great film-makers, Buñuel transforms every subject he touches. More importantly, even when subjected to the pressures of the film industry, he has never betrayed his deepest artistic and personal convictions; he has always seized every opportunity to reaffirm (usually via insinuation rather than in the outright way likely to shock the sensibilities of political and Christian censors) the very same message that emerged with such force from his first films.

This proud, uncompromising attitude of Buñuel's is shared by only a very few contemporary film-makers, who remain similarly true to themselves and for whom the idea of prostituting their talent is absolutely unthinkable.

Buñuel's admirable moral incorruptibility is almost certainly due to the fact that he does not place the cinema on a pedestal. For him, it is not an absolute language to which, as if to some sacred cow, all must be sacrificed in order to gain the fleeting plaudits of a tiny circle of *cinéphiles*. He has always been fully aware of the relative importance of film-making, and has always unhesitatingly stated that the act of living is far more important than fame, aesthetics or semiology, and that a film is simply a complement of conversation—a way of provoking thought via praxis, and a stimulating means of communication rather than an object to be savoured at leisure by the semanticians who will flock to the *cinémathèques* of the future. In an interview with Yvonne Baby[11], Buñuel said: "I wouldn't want to go on making films just in order to make a living. If I have only one year left to live, then I'm wasting my time with the cinema. I want to enjoy life, not to work; I want to see my friends, to eat, to drink, or just to sit quietly in my room watching the flies buzzing around or looking at the toes of my shoes. Quite seriously, the aim of the cinema strikes me as rather ridiculous, and I'm not interested in producing anything sublime."

Buñuel's quiet strength, his deliberate unwillingness to get caught up in the competitive rat-race that enables third-rate film critics to fill the bookshelves of libraries with works that treat the cinema as though it were a steeplechase, and his openness of spirit to everything that is mysterious, funny, painful or unjust in the world—all these qualities go to explain his basic commitment as a man amongst men. Buñuel has never felt the need to draw attention to himself socially or otherwise, which explains his unsensational private life and a human contact that always makes a great impression on those who meet him for the first time: "The man who is now coming down the stairs is tall. His hair and his moustache are dark, his eyes watchful and gentle. The first thing that strikes one (and it is an impression that lingers on) is the tenderness and the youthfulness that emanate from Buñuel. One would never imagine he was sixty-two. Buñuel explained that he lived a retiring, almost isolated life, within his own universe. He does not like travelling, least of all by plane. 'Not because of one's fear of death—that goes without saying—but because one feels a sense of anguish when one realises that one's up there in the sky, with nothing to do.' "[12]

★ ★ ★

In order to restore to man his carnal and terrestrial salvation, it is first necessary to reject (through ridicule rather than logical argument) the red herring of religious ecstasy, and to transform a society which, whether it be bourgeois or pseudo-socialist, is based on hypocrisy. But in order to be able to change it one must not only know it but be able to, and have the courage to, unmask its cunning alienation techniques. One must show how social injustice injures psychological make-up, or, if you prefer, one should only involve psychology within a given situation (in Sartre's sense of the word) and thus unravel the tangled skein that leads to one of the roads to freedom. This is precisely Buñuel's method, and it is this that sets him apart from film-makers who are vulnerable to the blandishments of metaphysics—the most characteristic of these being Fellini, Bresson, Rossellini and Dreyer (Bergman, too, up until *Persona*, but to a lesser degree). These directors, like the high-priests of Moral Rearmament, Billy Graham's emulators, and even Christians in general, believe that the "inner life" of individuals (who refuse the grace of God, then thirst for it and are comforted by it) is the greatest fact of human life, and that it can be

47

used in some magical way to transform a world of injustice, exploitation and suffering.

Buñuel will have none of this mystifying mumbo-jumbo. For him there is no transcendental road to salvation via the vale of tears. The only things that matter are man himself and the emotions he experiences.

This sort of truth is more difficult to express in the cinema than elsewhere. Film-makers have to accept the conditions imposed by governing bodies; either they must shut up and be out of a job, or resort to subterfuge in saying what they want to say. Buñuel in Mexico chose the latter course. From the very start he sincerely picked up the thread of the ideas in his first films; but as he was forced to adopt a slightly less frenzied tone, one which less suited his Spanish temperament, he occasionally lapsed into ambiguity and did not always succeed in injecting just the right dose of venom into a form which had to be, at least on the surface, traditional. Sometimes only a hint of what he is trying to say is detectable in the welter of melodrama. But his atheism, although quietly self-assured in a way that strongly contrasts with the violent destructiveness of his first films, is just as virulent as before when it comes to attacking the church.

Los Olvidados is by far the most important of the films Buñuel was to make before *El*. It deals with the problem of juvenile delinquency in the suburbs of a large city. It is in fact set in Mexico City, but the situation could apply equally well to New York, Rome, London or Paris. Buñuel shows how social conditions, lack of affection and poverty can turn a child into a criminal. The film is simply a record, and attempts to find no solution to the problem. As the introductory commentary puts it, "we leave the forces of progress to find a solution."

The delinquents live in shacks. Completely left to their own devices, they form gangs; under the leadership of Jaibo, a sinister young hood who has just escaped from reform school, they attempt to rob a blind street musician. Then, in the course of paying off an old score, Jaibo brutally murders Julian in the presence of Pedro. An unspoken complicity springs up between the two adolescents. Pedro is both fascinated and frightened by Jaibo, who takes advantage of the situation, hounds him to the knife works where he has found a job and then to the reform school. In his determination to drag Pedro down with him, Jaibo kills him in a fit of madness and is himself shot by the police.

The twists and turns of the plot enable Buñuel to describe in a vivid way the boys' relationship with each other, with their parents, with the police and with their educators. But he is not concerned with putting across a thesis about rehabilitation methods; his whole film is on a different level from Delannoy's self-indulgent *Chiens perdus sans collier,* Truffaut's autobiographical *Les 400 Coups,* the facile optimism of Nikolai Ekk's *The Way to Life* and Donskoi and Legoshin's *Song of Happiness,* or the repulsive sentimentality of all those films that bring tears to the eyes of the charitable by depicting the plight of waifs and strays. Even so, *Los Olvidados* is but a pale reflection of the unbearable objectivity and irrefutable indictment to be found in *Las Hurdes.* Buñuel does not manage to avoid rather romanticising the reform school, whereas he knows full well that it is no more than a plaster cast on a wooden leg. Economic and religious causes are merely hinted at, and the behaviour of the characters seems to move rather arbitrarily from paroxysm to paroxysm. This lack of balance between the over-vivid colours of the description and the haziness of the critical content provoked the following remark by Georges Franju after a projection of *Los Olvidados:* "It is not a *violent* film; it is simply *brutal* from time to time." The difference between "violent" and "brutal" is far from negligible. Maybe Buñuel thought he could replace one by the other; but in the process the film lost some of its fundamental impact. In spite of this flaw, however, it does contain some admirable sequences. And the fact that it steers clear of any suggestion of manicheism lends it a disturbing complexity and a poetic inspiration that abounds in searing images. The poor old blind man likes young boys, well-dressed queers flit along shopfronts, the grandfather prefers to dump his grandson's corpse on the rubbish tip (the *"chorrito"*) rather than having anything to do with the police, the hens and the cock seem literally to have an evil influence. There are images that are bursting with eroticism: a young girl pours milk on her thighs to soften her skin, two hands caress the naked back of a sick woman with a dove. In a dream, one of the children has a vision of his mother proffering him a hunk of the meat she refused to let him eat; the mangy dog of death scurries past.

Photographed by Figueroa without any seeking after effect (at Buñuel's express instructions) this love poem about those deprived of love achieves a visual and emotional conjugation of cruelty and tenderness. Jacquer Prévert put it this way, at the beginning of a prose poem he wrote in homage to the film[13]:

> Los Olvidados
> children that love and are not loved
> adolescent murderers
> murdered . . .

★ ★ ★

Los Olvidados won the prize for best direction at the 1951 Cannes Film Festival, and when the film came out in Paris its distributor produced a little brochure of enthusiastic press cuttings. In it, Jean Cocteau (who also did the drawing for the cover) wrote: "When Rossini was asked who was the greatest musician, he replied: Beethoven. And when his questioner said: 'And what about Mozart?', he replied: 'You asked me who was the greatest; you didn't ask me who was unique.' Buñuel is unique. His film is a masterpiece."

There is not much to be said about the minor works that preceded *El* and *Robinson Crusoe*, except for *Subida al Cielo* and, at

The blind man and his temptation in LOS OLVIDADOS

a pinch, *Susana* and *El Bruto,* films which Buñuel himself does not consider very highly but which have been overestimated by some commentators, who tend to see hidden meanings in every shot.

La Hija del Engano (or *Don Quintin el Amargao*), is a remake of Luis Marquina's film of 1935, on which Buñuel was executive producer (and which J. F. Aranda, in spite of what the credit titles say, believes to have been directed by Buñuel). The scenario is a melodrama in the best *Fanny by Gaslight* tradition: Don Quintin is an extremely honest little white-collar worker who admits from the very start: "Nothing I do turns out right." His wife is unfaithful. When he kicks her out, she reveals that he is not the father of their young daughter, Marta. He therefore decides to entrust the child to Lencho, a drunkard, and his wife, who agree to bring her up with their own daughter, Jovita, who is of the same age. From that moment on, Don Quintin becomes short-tempered, vicious and embittered. He owns a cabaret. When his wife, just before dying, confesses that Marta is in fact his own child, he sets out to find her. But years have passed meanwhile. Marta has grown up, left her adoptive parents, and married her boy friend, Paco. Don Quintin gives Jovita star billing in the hope that Marta will come and applaud her performance. But meanwhile Don Quintin and Paco cross swords, and it looks as though their quarrel will end in bloodshed. But when Don Quintin discovers that Paco is his daughter's husband, he is so happy that he buries the hatchet: "Marta!"—"Daddy!"

"Happiness makes me a better man," admits Don Quintin when he is told he is a grandfather. When he expresses the desire to see his grandson immediately, he is told that the child has not yet been born. "You see? Nothing I do turns out right!", he says impishly at the end of the film, looking straight at the camera.

Buñuel does not allow himself the luxury of indulging in a crude, caricatural piece of parody. He keeps strictly within the conventions of Mexican melodrama, but from time to time livens things up with just a slight piece of emphasis or a moment of wry understatement. We see, for instance, Marta as a little girl in Lencho's house. There is a black-out for several seconds on the screen, and all we hear is the spanking Marta is getting from the drunkard. When the picture comes back Marta is now a young woman. The dialogue informs us that Lencho still spanks her, but the significance of this corporal punishment has of course changed: there is now a strong erotic element in it. In this way, Buñuel guides us almost imperceptibly from a *cliché* situation (step-father versus poor waif) to the phenomenological description of an emotional relationship that is based on a reciprocal, instinctive and unstoppable quest for pleasure. All through the film, Buñuel pulls out the stops of sentimentality with such abandon that the result is humour or irony; and through some pataphysical logic, the fatuously edifying plot of the film suddenly debunks itself.

Buñuel uses the same device in *Susana* and in *El Bruto*, but does so with even greater success in *El*. This kind of exaggerated dramatisation, aimed at disparaging the ideology it at first sight seems to be illustrating, has often been used in the cinema, without direct reference to Brecht. One could quote countless examples, from Petrov's *The Storm* (1934) to *Three Sad Tigers* (1968), by the Chilean director, Raúl Ruiz.

The young and beautiful Susana is terrified by the various fauna that seem to be sharing her dingy cell in the reform school where she has been sent for sinning while still under age. She beseeches God to give her some means of escaping from her woeful lot. Then she goes up to the bars of her cell and, by some miracle, prises them apart with the greatest of ease. Lashed by wind and rain, she escapes into the countryside where she finds refuge with a rich landowner and his peaceful family, who lose no time in putting into practice all the precepts of Christian charity. Susana cunningly uses her stunning beauty as a weapon, and seizes every opportunity to titillate, hoisting up her skirt in the course of her domestic chores or nonchalantly leaning forward to show her plunging neckline to advantage. Her first conquest is Jesus, the overseer, who gets her in a clinch as she is walking back from the hen-house with her apron full of eggs (result: a nice shot of goo-covered thighs). Then she gets to work on the son of the house, seducing him away from his study of grasshoppers and other insects. And finally she makes advances to the father, Don Guadelupe, a worthy gentleman who has to draw on all the moral strength he derives from religion in order to resist her. But before long he too weakens and gives in. His wife, Doña Carmena, is furious and wants to send the intruder packing. The men, out of jealousy, come to hate each other, and it looks very much as though the film will end with a bloodbath. But Jesus finds out about Susana's past, and betrays her to the police, who come to take her back to prison. Everything slips back into place. Everybody resumes their *façade* of respect for the catechism and for propriety. But the whole point of Buñuel's cautionary tale is to bring out the oppressiveness and flimsiness of such a moral code.

El Bruto, which was shot very rapidly (eighteen days) like most of Buñuel's minor Mexican films, could have carried a stronger social punch than the bucolic *Susana.* Certainly the film's setting (in a large city, with a background of capitalist exploitation in the horrible world of slaughterhouses, where a statue of the Virgin Mary quietly looks down from above the gates) is effective.

Pedro is a young butcher who has been most appositely nicknamed "the brute." A big property owner, on the advice of his wife, Paloma, takes on Pedro as a strong-arm man to deal with tenants who have fallen behind with their rent. With a single back-handed blow of his hand Pedro kills a worker called Carmelo, who has been one of the most vociferous in protesting against the unjust way Cabrera has been calling for the eviction of the poor. Paloma is deeply impressed by the physical strength of this hired killer, and becomes his mistress. Pedro is chased, and wounded, by tenants who want to avenge Carmelo's death; he takes refuge with the daughter of the dead man, Meche, who is of course unaware that the man she is looking after is her father's murderer. Pedro begins to live with Meche, and becomes a gentler, more approachable human being. He starts regretting his shameful, criminal past, and feels sympathy for the miserable victims of Cabrera. But Paloma is vexed by this redemptive love; in a fit of jealousy she sets her husband against Pedro and reveals the truth to the unsuspecting Meche. The latter breaks off with Pedro, who, in a blind fury, strangles Cabrera after having pinned him down on a table, of which all we see, at the height of their struggle, are its shaking legs. Paloma then denounces Pedro to the police, who shoot him down just as Meche is forgiving him.

As far as the direction is concerned, *El Bruto* is an excellently made film that bristles with very Buñuelesque personal touches. Ado Kyrou has called it a "superb melodrama," but it is also an extremely black film that contains more than a whiff of brimstone. In his interview with *Cahiers du Cinéma*,[14] Buñuel said: "*El Bruto* could have been a good film. The scenario I wrote with Alcoriza was quite interesting, but I was forced to change it completely. The result is pretty mediocre, and certainly nothing to shout about."

While *Los Olvidados* is nothing to laugh about, *Subida al Cielo* seems, at first sight at least, to be a jolly caper. But one should beware of taking it simply as a piece of run-of-the-mill vaudeville entertainment. It is rather like a box with a false bottom, and more than once what first seems to be frothy comedy turns out to be black humour. Take for instance the sequence in which the bus gets bogged down in the middle of a ford. A tractor alone is unable to budge it, so two oxen are harnessed to it in the hope that they will provide the extra energy needed for the success of the operation. Everybody is bustling around in preparation for this when suddenly the coach moves forward: the oxen are following a little girl who is leading them by a string. The relieved passengers clamber back into the vehicle, and it is only at the last moment that they see a man with a wooden leg who is stuck in the mud and calling for help.

The film is reminiscent not so much of Blasetti's *Quattro passi fra le nuvole* as of the happy-go-lucky voyagers of Pierre and Jacques Prévert's *Voyage Surprise:* both films possess the same wild, anarchic, and surrealist-inspired humour.

The plot hinges on an outward and a return journey in a bus. When the film opens, we are in a village which has no church (a happy village therefore) and where the inhabitants make a living from coconut palms ("a coconut palm," we are informed by the commentary, "is as profitable as a cow"). Oliverio has just married. He and his young wife are gliding over the water in a flower-

Buñuel gives a plastic tangibility to human flesh. From SUBIDA AL CIELO

decked boat and are preparing to consummate their union when a motor launch appears on the scene. He learns that his mother is dying and rushes to her bedside. She tells him that she intends to cut off her sons without a penny and make her young nephew Chuchito her heir. The only person she trusts is Oliverio who, unlike his brothers, does not covet the inheritance. So she asks him to travel into town in order to find a notary who can legally draw up her last will and testament. Meanwhile, the other brothers are having a booze-up with the mayor. They are just as drunk with the idea of coming into a fortune as with the alcohol: their mother's death agony becomes a reason for rejoicing, and one of them makes a remark that could well be a surrealist proverb: "One only has one mother and she only dies once!"

The town is very far away, and in order to get there one has to go over the mountains by a pass known as Subida al Cielo (Ascent into the Heavens). Preparations for the expedition get under way in the village square. People load the coach with luggage, which includes an oval mirror with a decorated frame (although an odd object to be found among the luggage, it is included as a piece of realistic local colour, and not simply through a desire to be bizarre at all costs). Then the passengers begin to arrive. There is an extremely wide range of characters (even not counting all the others who get on *en route*, with their sheep, young goats and hen-coops): a pregnant woman who gives birth during the journey, a candidate for public office who gets welcomed with a hail of stones by his electors, a vamp called Raquel (of the same type as Susana) who arouses strong desires in Oliverio (she hands him an apple, he crunches it, the world reels, he unbuttons Raquel's dress, and they lie down together in a bus that seems overgrown with weeds), and who later causes him to be unfaithful. There is also a fey bus-driver who makes a detour from the normal route in order to go and kiss his old mother who is celebrating her birthday at a nearby ranch. The stop-off at the ranch turns into a real hoe-down, with dancing and a banquet. Oliverio is here reminiscent of Meursault in Camus's *L'Etranger:* while he is dancing with Raquel, he might well, in all innocence, have forgotten his dying mother and forlorn wife. In the end, when all the passengers are seriously the worse for drink and the stop-off at the ranch looks like lasting a considerable time, Oliverio himself takes the wheel of the coach and sets off for town. But Raquel has managed to slip aboard with him; as they drive up the pass she makes advances to him, and they make love in the bus at the height of a mountain storm. On his arrival in town, Oliverio goes to see the notary, who pleading his old age regrets that he is unable to undertake the journey, but is willing to prepare all the necessary documents. As he hands them to the young man, he says: "Your mother need only append her fingerprint." Then begins the return journey, during which peasants who look as though they had stepped out of *Las Hurdes* wave down the coach and load on a small coffin containing the corpse of a little girl. "She was bitten by a viper," they remark. The vehicle stops in front of a cemetery, and all the passengers join in the funeral ceremony just as they had taken part in the birthday celebrations of the driver's mother.

When Oliverio gets back to his village, his mother has already died. He sees Raquel again in a dream; then he picks up his mother's lifeless hand, coats the thumb with ink, presses it on to the documents and meticulously cleans it. Finally, he returns to his wife and, now a liberated man, picks up his wedding night where he left off.

The surrealist poet, Benjamin Péret, has written of the film[24]: "Although *Subida al Cielo* does not allow Buñuel to give full expression to his torment as do some of his other films, it is still, in more than one respect, a very attaching film, if only because of the dream sequence during which the bus becomes a greenhouse where Lilia Prado knits potato peelings. The final scene, too, where the hero places his dead mother's thumbs on the will, is vintage Buñuel. This film, like all his others, is notable for the crispness of its direction and for the complete absence of any superfluous elements. It is presumably from the contrast between the intensity of his subjects and the restraint of his style that Buñuel derives most of his startling effects. All his films bear, to a varying degree, the imprint of the poet in revolt who first came to light with *L'Age d'Or* and *Las Hurdes;* for Buñuel has the eyes of a poet, and his pen is the camera."

In his interview with *Cahiers du Cinéma*,[15] Buñuel said: "I liked *Subida al Cielo* very much. I love the moments where nothing happens, like when the man says: 'Give me a match.' I'm very interested in that sort of thing. I'm fascinated by 'Give me a match' or 'Do you want to eat?' or 'What's the time?' I was thinking of that sort of thing when I made *Subida al Cielo*."

As with Picasso, Buñuel's tongue-in-cheek remarks are much more significant than they seem at first sight. His way, for instance, of showing keen interest in dialogue like "Give me a match" or in moments where nothing happens is simply a sign of his unfailing attention to just the sort of thing that is neglected by conventional directors, who are much more concerned with the aesthetico-dramatic significance that can be extracted from a given situation. Buñuel's prime preoccupation, however, is with creating an atmosphere, picking on a detail or a possibility of triggering off an excursion into fantasy, pulling aside almost imperceptibly the curtain of realism to reveal a parallel world, or allowing the narrative to run amok much in the same way as automatic writing. With seeming nonchalance, Buñuel cocks the gun of mystery. His extremely keen sensibility enables him to capture the unique quality of a silence, the infinity of a moment, or the vertigo of an emotion. His creative authority rests not on his skill as a dramatist but on a magic quality that is very reminiscent of Bachelard's *La Poétique et la Rêverie*. Bachelard and Buñuel have more than one point in common; and what Bachelard says of Lautréamont[16] could well be applied to Buñuel: "[This work] has no aim, it is an action. It has no plan, and it is coherent. Its language is not the expression of pre-existent thought. It is the expression of a psychic force that suddenly becomes a language. In short, it is instant language."

To return to *Subida al Cielo*, it should be remembered that the film's main characteristic, as Buñuel himself says, is the *joie de vivre* that went into the making of it. The director was no more interested in aesthetic theory than he was in the cardboard sets he was forced to use. It is almost as though Buñuel were sitting by a tinkling stream, dropping petals into it and thinking about nothing in particular, simply happy to be in the open air. His favourite themes (love, society, death) are there, but in this film at least they are treated in less serious vein. Love emerges the victor without too much difficulty because Oliverio is a healthy, natural person who has been brought up *in a village with no church*. He can allow himself to be guided by his instincts. He has not yet been irreparably contaminated by social taboos.

The same cannot be said of Francisco, the incurably sick hero of *El*. On the contrary, he is a man of the church who tries to use his social standing and his Christian faith to plaster over his unwholesome subconscious.

★ ★ ★

L'Age d'Or offers us a vertical cross-section of a society whose hypocrisy stifles love. *El* may be considered as the horizontal cross-section of the same society: Buñuel uses the inverse, negative process, and eliminates the elements of revolt, scandal and insult. But although his attack on established values in *El* may seem more insidious it is nonetheless just as hardhitting as *L'Age d'Or*. The hero played by Modot in the earlier film here becomes Arturo de Cordova, an anti-hero, a willing victim of, and accessory to, the political, economic and religious establishment: he is a Hurdano in a dinner jacket, or a Majorcan, if you like.

It would be a great mistake to try and see this film solely as a study of a pathological case. For the case in question is set in a context that explains it and is explicable through it. Francisco's jealousy is not a cut-and-dried emotion that can be neatly slotted into a psychological pigeonhole; it is one of the many aspects of the behaviour of a man who is produced by his milieu as much as he himself produces it. His jealousy is an unconscious urge both to rid himself of tension and symbolically to mask his impotence; in addition the careful spectator will see a clear parallel between the jealous individual (Francisco) and the debasement of the world that conditions his behaviour (a class society).

The opening sequence is as delicious as the founding of Rome in *L'Age d'Or*. We are in a church on Maundy Thursday. A priest washes and kisses the feet of a dozen adolescents, who seem utterly bored with the ceremony. Francisco, who is officiating behind the padre, allows his eyes to linger on each kiss. Then his gaze travels from the boy's bare feet to the congregation's footwear, and we see a pretty pair of silk-stockinged, high-arched feet in high-heeled shoes. His eyes run up curvaceous legs towards the face of a beautiful, unknown woman, who is staring at him. After the service, he tries to meet her, but without success. She continues, however, to obsess him.

Who exactly is Francisco? A rich landlord in his forties who is currently embroiled in a court case. He feels that his lawyer is not being tough enough, and dismisses him. He is a bachelor with quite inflexible views regarding the principles of Christian morality, and is therefore still a virgin. He is a firm believer in Law, Justice and Duty (or, if you like, the Vichy formula of Work, Family and Country). Like Modot, he could be an influential member of the International Charity Organisation. He feels happy in his villa (a kind of poor man's Xanadu), which is an architectural mess and is cluttered up with things his grandfather brought back from the 1900 Exposition Universelle in Paris. Francisco cannot bear a picture to be lopsided and baulks at his manservant sleeping with the chambermaid. "I will not have this sort of thing in my house. The girl must go!" The fact that he kicks out the girl and not Pablo, the manservant, is fairly typical of the defensive way he reacts to members of the fair sex, but it also reflects the arrogant self-confidence and tacit understanding that is the very foundation of men's presumptuous domination in bourgeois society.

Whenever his court case gives him a little respite, his mind races feverishly back to the unknown woman. He goes to church every day, as before, but now he is spurred on solely by the hope of seeing her again: he has heard the first call of freedom. His piety is completely degraded by his desire—proof, if one were needed, that desire and love are stronger and more worthwhile than religion. One day, he catches sight of her again, follows her in a taxi, spies on her through a restaurant window, and realises she is engaged to an engineer he knows called Raoul. So he finds some trifling pretext to call on Raoul, and learns that he plans to marry Gloria. Francisco seizes this opportunity: "Come round to dinner. Come with your *fiancée* and her mother. I'll chat up the mother," he quips with a smile. Raoul accepts the invitation.

Francisco has prepared the evening down to the last detail. He showers attentions on Gloria, talks of falling madly in love, drops heavy hints, and explains his theory of how to seduce women while the priest chuckles with delight as he stuffs himself with turkey and Pablo sends clouds of dust into the room from an adjoining store-room where he is moving furniture—an obvious reminder of the smoke that escapes from the kitchen in *L'Age d'Or*. No ox-drawn cart rumbles across the room, but one feels it might at any moment, just as one does during the hoity-toity "at home" in *Cela s'appelle l'aurore*. Like Modot and Lya Lys, Francisco and Gloria slip into the statue-strewn garden, where they kiss for the first time. Then there is suddenly an abrupt cut: we see an explosion in the side of a mountain, and Raoul poring over the plans of a dam. When a colleague remarks that they will have to go down into town, Raoul says, in a weary, disillusioned way: "Mexico City no longer means anything to me." This eloquent short-cut enables Buñuel not only to fill in much of the plot by suggestion (Francisco has taken over Raoul's role), but to turn the spectator's attention immediately on to the behaviour of Francisco towards the woman of his dreams.

In the first of a series of flashbacks, Gloria herself describes her husband's morbid fixations. She starts with an account of their honeymoon.

On their wedding night in a sleeping car, Francisco badgers her with questions ("A penny for your thoughts." "I'm thinking of you." "No you're not, you liar. . . ."). He grovels at her feet, then insults her, then beseeches forgiveness, skipping agilely from masochism to sadism. The town that Francisco has chosen for their honeymoon is one that enables him to feel king of the castle: "This is the home-town of my family." He almost gives the impression of owning the whole place, and takes great pleasure in using his wealth to make his wife feel small and even in incorporating her, like some prize antique, in his panoply of possessions and property. While on a stroll, the newly-weds bump into a certain Ricardo, a roly-poly talkative character that Gloria has known slightly for some time. Francisco jumps to the conclusion that Ricardo has once been Gloria's lover—a supposition that is quite patently absurd. After lengthy discussion, Francisco admits that his suspicions were unfounded, and when he calms down Gloria

Francisco, like Modot in L'AGE D'OR, is held back in the street in EL

says to him almost shyly: "Sometimes you're unfair." This angers him, and he retorts: "Few people are as aware as myself of what is fair or unfair." Shortly afterwards, he again falls victim to a fit of jealousy when they once again meet Ricardo in the hotel restaurant: "He's following you . . . He's watching you . . . He's laughing . . . He thinks it's all a great joke . . .", Francisco shouts accusingly at Gloria. Then he makes a scene, and asks for their meal to be brought up to their room. A little later he discovers, while putting his shoes in the corridor to be cleaned, that Ricardo is staying in the next room. He really loses his temper: "I come back to my birthplace, and this fellow starts spying on my private life." He creeps up to the door, inserts a knitting needle into the keyhole, and with a sharp thrust hopes somehow to get the voyeur in the eye. Of course there is nobody there when he opens the door, simply because Ricardo could not care two hoots about Gloria or her husband. But Francisco is not to be deterred: he gets more and more worked up, buttonholes Ricardo, slaps him on the face, and ends up by getting him thrown out of the hotel. "After three forlorn weeks we returned to Mexico City."

Gloria then gives us another instalment of the misfortunes of her virtue. During a party for Gloria's birthday, Francisco literally throws her into the arms of a lawyer: "Be nice to him, I must win my case!" Obedient as ever, she dances with him and makes herself thoroughly pleasant to him. When the guests have gone home he accuses her of having been too familiar. Next day, as he bends down, he notices Gloria's feet under the table and is filled with desire: he smothers her with kisses. She says to him wearily: "Leave me alone." His sexual hunger changes in a flash to anger: "That's not the way you'd speak to your lawyer friend, is it?" He insults her, and takes the servants to witness; throughout the following night the silence of the house is shattered by Gloria's cries. Gloria decides to go and weep on her mother's shoulder; but the latter rushes to her son-in-law's defence (he has already come and told her that Gloria is a good girl at heart who needs the occasional ticking off), and sends her back to her husband, adding in maternal fashion: "Be understanding." Gloria is disappointed, and turns to the priest, who also tries to convince her that she alone is in the wrong: "Francisco's soul holds no secrets for me. He has already unbosomed himself to me. He is without sin." When she goes back home, Francisco is waiting for her, pistol in hand. He fires and she falls. We then move to Raoul's car, and Gloria says: "It had a blank cartridge in it! After that, Francisco became normal again; but this morning. . . ." And she goes on with her story, which Buñuel then describes visually.

Francisco is on the telephone and gets worked up about his court case. Then he asks Gloria nicely if she would like to go for a walk with him: "I know a wonderful place to go!" He takes her up to the top of a bell-tower, and says, as he looks down on the crowds of people below: "When I come up this high, I begin to live. I would like to squash those crawling insects. Mankind inspires me with contempt. I could give you the punishment you deserve . . ." He leaps on her and tries to throw her over the parapet. She manages to escape, and the narrative shifts back once and for all into the present, with Gloria in Raoul's car. Raoul says: "You delight in suffering, otherwise you'd have left him. Get yourself a lawyer. Give me a ring if you want to." They draw up in front of the house. Francisco sees them from far away without being able to recognise the man with her. "Who was it?" he asks the moment she comes in. "Raoul." "You slut!" He goes into a rage, stamps his feet like a spoilt child and goes to sulk in Pablo's room; he finds his valet in bed surrounded by the various parts of a bicycle he has taken to pieces, and says: "I'm so unhappy, my wife is being unfaithful to me."

During the night he wanders through the house like a caged animal, zigzags his way up the stairs, then sits on one of the steps, pulls out one of the rods that hold the carpet in place and drums it frantically against the banisters. The sound is a clear reminder of the drums in *L'Age d'Or* and foreshadows the drums that make the ambiguity of *Nazarin* quite unequivocal.

Francisco's married life continues to shift from one extreme to the other—from bottled up *amour fou* to insane hatred. One night, while everybody is asleep, he prepares the ultimate outrage: he is going to sew up Gloria, just as in the last lesson of Sade's *La Philosophie dans le Boudoir* Eugénie, Dolmance and Madame de Saint-Ange sew up Madame de Mistival's orifices with a needle and red thread. In his interview with *Cahiers du Cinéma*, Buñuel explains himself: "I had no explicit intention of imitating Sade in my choice of elements, but it is quite possible that I did so unconsciously. It's natural for me to tend to imagine and work out a situation from a Sadist or Sade-like point of view rather than from, say, a neo-realist or mystical one. I said to myself: what should the character use? A revolver? A knife? A chair? I ended up by choosing the most disturbing objects. It's as simple as that." Francisco calmly gets together a bottle, some cotton, a pair of scissors, a rope, some razor blades, an awl and some thread. But Gloria wakes up with a start and manages to escape him. "I know where she is." He rushes to Raoul's house, where a maidservant tells him that her master has just gone out. He darts back into the street, spots Raoul, follows him, leaps into a taxi when he thinks he sees Gloria in a passing car, follows her, arrives at a church, enters, and recognises, from behind, Raoul and Gloria side by side in the front row of pews. The priest intones Mass, and Francisco falls to his knees. A little old man with a goatee coughs near him. This cough triggers off a fit of hallucinatory madness in Francisco, the first symptoms of which had become apparent during the early part of the sequence. For a split second in his eyes, the congregation seems to be laughing, then continues it prayers normally. The couple in the first row are not of course Raoul and Gloria but two people who look like them. A meditating woman guffaws, then abruptly resumes her serious expression. The priest conducting the service suddenly makes a grimace in between two perfectly normal movements. The choirboys cock snooks at him, then imperturbably follow the service. The marvellous editing of this whole sequence is informed with a quite extraordinary destructive energy. In this way, the phenomenon of worship is not caricaturised: it is shattered from within. Vital forces burst out from its straitjacket just as wine spurts from a leaking barrel. Surface appearances give way to the reality that lies behind them. Francisco cannot bear these home truths: he springs on the priest and tries to strangle him in front of the altar. He is overpowered by members of the congregation, and order is restored.

A car draws up in front of a monastery. Time has elapsed. We see Gloria, Raoul, and their son, who is about ten years old. They are talking to the head of the monastery, and ask for news about Brother Francisco. "He is gentle and humble. His behaviour is quite exemplary. You can see him if you wish. It wouldn't make him suffer—he is protected from his past by his faith." Gloria, Raoul and their son (whom they have called Francisco) leave. The head of the monastery goes up to Brother Francisco, who looks up from beneath his hood and asks: "Have they gone?" He is answered with a nod. He then adds: "My madness was nothing serious. The past is dead. Once again I am a serene man." And the film ends with his zigzagging his way down an alleyway of the garden, echoing his behaviour at the height of his madness—an absolutely brilliant visual idea that is typical of the whole film. *El*, which manages to assimilate rather than rebel against the daunting commercial pressures under which it was made, is nothing more or less than a masterpiece.

The long summary of the film's melodramatic plot which I have just given should make it clear that its highlights of jealousy and foot fetishism conceal a subtly constructed piece of psycho-social criticism that unmasks exactly the same oppressive set-up as that described in *L'Age d'Or*. But in *El* the motivations for the hero's failure in love are more fully emphasised. As Robert Benayoun wrote, in *Le Nouvel Observateur* of December 10, 1964, "Buñuel goes further and shows that the idea of God" (the only wrong, according to Sade, for which he could not forgive humanity) "crushes mankind." Whereas Modot opts for rebellion, Francisco chooses to inflict upon himself a conventional, repressed pattern of behaviour that results, during the sequence, for instance, where he is unable to dictate a letter to Gloria, in a typical manifestation of impotence. Whereas Modot's desire leads him openly to cause scandals and to trample on all established values (to slap wheedling matrons, kick blind men, jeer at pity, insult ministers and put sex before everything), Francisco's urges are caught in a vicious circle, disintegrate, and seethe in the pressure cooker of religious and bourgeois principles. And yet although consistent self-denial results in the gradual stifling of desire, which finally seems to be tamed and completely sublimated in the person of the serene, secluded monk, one should not imagine that this desire has been totally annihilated. For however great the alienation, however powerful the institutional regulations aimed at damping it, love never loses its faculty of suddenly bursting out. This is why the uneasy conscience continually strives to escape the ever-present, ever-watchful threat of love by seeking refuge in mysticism. One might almost adapt Sartre's remark about Mauriac's conception of carnal love (that "carnal love is love of God that has gone astray"), and say that to love God is to lead astray the love of man—to "Hurdanise" it so it can only result in a monastic neurosis and utter cretinisation. "Often the only motive in becoming a nun or a monk is self-protection from the sort of encounters that might disrupt a deep-rooted complex. First of all an unattainable love is replaced by a more abstract and more general love that takes place purely on a dream level. And then the person who has taken refuge from the world in this way vigorously barricades himself against the allurements of life outside, which he feels unable to tackle without running great risks. So the transition is made from love of one's father to love of Jesus, and love of one's mother to love of the Virgin Mary. This continual interrelation between the Oedipus complex and the call of mysticism is too obvious for one to need to stress it any further."[17]

The man who wrote those words, Pierre Mabille (in his book *Thérèse de Lisieux*), displays a startling affinity with the moral, spiritual, intellectual and political position of Buñuel from his first film to his last. Mabille says elsewhere: "I declare that the first step towards changing the future must be to abolish the existence of a supernatural, immaterial or divine love. The presence of the myth of Christ should disappear. Jesus' corpse must no longer come between man and woman. The image of a living man, who has been rewarded by his own effort and is aware of his own power, must supplant that of the poor wretch doomed to imperfection which the Church has been putting over for centuries. The illusory depiction of a heavenly perfection that can never be verified must now give way to a clear description of a reality which reveals itself daily to have greater and greater possibilities, so long as it is not disowned."[18]

A disillusioned Dan O'Herlihy in ROBINSON CRUSOE

From Loneliness to Friendship

In *Robinson Crusoe* Buñuel treats two themes—loneliness and friendship—in two distinct phases. He has always dreamt of describing man with all the cool objectivity of an entomologist poring over his specimen, but with an objectivity that stems from a strong desire for knowledge. He is always concerned with getting to know his characters better in order better to judge what he considers to be their vices and virtues. And so Buñuel is necessarily a moralist; but ethics begin to have a meaning for him only when they sweep away the values laid down by Church, School and Army. Robinson Crusoe was, therefore, an excellent subject for study. (Buñuel has said: "I didn't like the novel, but I did like the character of Crusoe.")

Here we have a man who finds himself in a situation where conventions no longer apply. He has been stripped of his social position and reduced to a kind of ontological purity: his desire to live and his fear of death can no longer be seen in terms of traditional morality. All that remains is a vague metaphysical uneasiness, which gradually becomes weaker and weaker, disappearing entirely in the overwhelming sequence where Crusoe calls to God and gets, as his only answer, the echo of his own voice; then panics, shouts for help, and in the twilight sadly throws his torch into the sea. From that moment on, he has won. He has put his existence to all the tests of a freedom that is devoid of cumbersome laws and rituals, and has emerged reborn.

Although featuring only a single character, the first part of the film does not come across as a self-consciously virtuoso piece of acting or directing. With warmhearted straightforwardness, Buñuel describes the mastering of oneself through asceticism (a return to a Rousseau-like state of ingenuousness) and through a gradual instrumental grasping of the world around one.

All this takes place against a background of completely "vegetalised" natural scenery: the bird calls, the silence, the rain, the sea and the sky seem to fuse into a huge green poem. Nature is used in the same way as it is in *La Mort en ce jardin,* as well as in *The African Queen, Heaven Knows Mr Allyson, Moby Dick* and *The Roots of Heaven.* For both Huston and Buñuel, man's organic relationship with the greenery around him does not mean he should sink into some pantheistic reverie, but rather makes explicit his negativity by offering him a means of combating both the blind force of rising sap (a kind of sticky evil which because of its ambivalence can be turned to the good either through the use of tools or through passion) and simultaneously God himself (an absolute evil that cannot be converted even through knowledge). It is only after the cry "God is dead" that man is able to exclaim: "I can see."

Crusoe rescues from the wreck of his ship five or six chests, some guns, a telescope, a Bible, some medical supplies, a handful of grain, and sacks of gold sovereigns, discovering in the process that a little grain is more valuable than all the gold in the world. As the days go by, Crusoe begins to organise himself. He talks to his dog and is delighted when his cat has kittens. The corn ripens, but it looks dangerously as though it will be eaten by birds; so Crusoe makes a scarecrow out of a woman's dress. Suddenly it becomes obvious that he hankers for love and sex. He learns how to kindle a fire, knead dough, bake bread and throw a clay pot. He finds he has to fight against death, which threatens him in the form of a fever, and against the grief he feels at the death of his dog. He reads the Bible; but the scriptures no longer have any meaning for him.

After this first section of the film, where Crusoe learns how to come to terms with himself, there is the arrival of Man Friday and the problems of creating brotherhood. This rather new theme for Buñuel forms quite a neat complement to his usual twin motifs of revolt and love. One morning while walking along the beach,

Crusoe comes across a footprint larger than his own. This causes him a good deal of concern. In the end, he meets Man Friday. The impact of this newcomer on the recluse makes him recoil most dramatically: Crusoe creeps back into the shell of his former principles and forgets all that he has painfully learnt about himself. He becomes a "civilised" man again, takes on the role of the coloniser, and can only envisage his relationship with Man Friday as being that of master and slave. "At last I had found a servant again. I taught him to respect me with my musket." He puts irons on him and, a little later, teaches him Christian theology. But Man Friday reacts with quite disconcerting wisdom, which Buñuel sardonically compares to Sade's dying man, who retorts to the priest: "So your God was determined to make a mess of things just in order to be able to tempt his creation, or to put him to the test; didn't he know him any better? Surely he can't have been in any doubts about what the result would be?"[19]

Finally, then, it is Man Friday who, paradoxically enough, restores Crusoe's freedom—the freedom of a man who does not feel he has to dominate. Gradually their relationship eases its way towards mutual gratitude.

What will become of their friendship when they arrive in England is of course another matter. It is highly likely that Christian civilisation will rapidly make them forget the fruits of their common experience. For the story of Robinson Crusoe as told by Buñuel teaches us that, although man is free to free himself, his freedom remains extremely precarious. It can endure only if it is in a constant state of renewal, and is in constant danger of being fossilised by so-called "eternal" values that have been mummified by social myths and by a worship of the cultural past, of religion, and of political dogmatism.

Buñuel was particularly active during 1952 and 1953, making, one after the other, *El Bruto, Robinson Crusoe, El, Abismos de Pasión* and *La Ilusion Viaja en Tranvía*. The latter film and the one he made after it (*El Río y la Muerte*) were worth no more than a passing mention.

La Ilusión Viaja en Tranvía tells the story of two young employees of a municipal public transport company—driver and a conductor—who, because they are angry that their bosses have decided to withdraw an old tram on which they have worked for several years, decide, after a popular festival during which they have had a little too much to drink, to take the old girl on one last trip through the town. This results in a number of hilarious incidents and unexpected adventures, such as finding a sewing machine and an umbrella on a dissecting table. Buñuel takes this opportunity to describe certain aspects of the streets of Mexico City that are not to be found in travel brochures. The two chums have to slip through the traffic on routes that they know the regular timetable leaves free, and also have to keep their wild excursion going till nightfall, at which time they hope to drive the vehicle secretly back into the depot. The tram, which for *no reason at all* is launched on to a network of routes that has been meticulously worked out by the company's technocrats, becomes an element of joyful anarchy. Passengers waiting at stops fail to understand why they should not board the vehicle, and those who do so cannot see how they can travel without buying a ticket. As they have been completely conditioned by money, they are all mistrustful of this free public service and find plausible reasons for paying all the same. Buñuel thus heaps ridicule on our habits, and points an accusing finger at the sort of reflexes that our education has inculcated in us.

El Río y la Muerte (*The River of Death*) I have not seen myself. But Jean Delmas, in his magazine *Jeune Cinéma*, describes it quite fairly, I would have thought, in the following terms: "It is a film about a village vendetta between two families. It shows how it is almost impossible to escape a vitiated law that is based on a vitiated sense of honour, both for the woman who originally wanted to keep her son out of the whole murderous business, and even for the son, who has become a doctor and knows that his job is to save lives, not to take them. It may be legitimately feared that in France the film will be taken as a kind of joke or parody, because at times the scene of robot-like killing has the rhythm not of a Western, but of a parody of a Western. But I don't think that here Buñuel wanted to have a laugh; I believe he wanted to convince. For his Mexican audience, the meaning of the revolver shots is: 'Look! You let the other person have it just for a question of yes or no. Can't you see what a fool you look?' I think we would be wrong to laugh at this respect for science, which contrasts the doctor who saves lives with prejudices that cause death as though it were the result of mere naiveté. I am perfectly aware that Buñuel is more convincing when he limits himself to merely observing reality; but I would like to think that he agreed to make himself useful, like a village teacher, in the country he had adopted."[20]

Buñuel says only a few words about this film and the one that preceded it in his interview with *Cahiers du Cinéma* in 1954, and does not explicitly accept the pedagogic qualities that are eagerly read into his works by all his interpreters. He prefers to see himself rather as a craftsman, or even as an amused dabbler, because he knows very well that his films speak for themselves: "*La Ilusion Viaja en Tranvía* . . . the story of a tram stolen by two workers . . . they set out from a café and drive round the town in the stolen tram . . . there is one rather interesting reel in the film . . . *El Río y la Muerte* is about death Mexican-style, an 'easy death' . . . you know when a man has died, the place is full of people smoking and knocking back glasses of spirits . . . life is a very trifling thing, and death hardly counts at all. The film includes seven deaths, four funerals and umpteen vigils over the dead."[21]

Arcibaldo de la Cruz

Crusoe's bid for freedom, as well as Modot's in *L'Age d'Or*, are echoed in an apparently lighter vein in the story of Arcibaldo de la Cruz, a character who closely resembles Francisco in *El* and Viridiana's uncle, *Don Jaime*. The difference is that he manages to overcome his inhibitions and salvage his emotional urges from the quagmire of an oversexed libido. "I am frightened by my aspirations," he admits at one point. "Sometimes I thirst to be a great saint, while at others I almost feel I could become a notorious criminal." Fortunately for him, he ends up by simply becoming a free man—something far more difficult and praiseworthy in a society like our own, of which he, like all of us, is a stunted product weighed down by two thousand years of Christianity.

The young Arcibaldo is a spoilt child who is smothered with lovely toys by his rich bourgeois parents. His favourite pastime is to hide in a huge cupboard and dress up in mummy's expensive clothes and underwear. We realise already that he could well end up mad, like Francisco, or like Don Jaime, whose wife died while still a virgin and whose wedding dress he religiously keeps in a chest like a holy relic.

One day, Arcibaldo's mother gives her darling little boy a musical box with a pretty mechanical ballerina on top. The child is told that this dainty automaton is just like one which was used by a certain king to make his most dangerous enemies magically disappear: all he had to do was think very hard about the death of an enemy and start up the music—and the enemy dropped dead. Arcibaldo immediately experiments on the maid, and in the twinkling of an eye she is hit in the head by a stray bullet (there happens to be a revolution taking place at just that very moment). She lies dead on the carpet, with her skirt hoisted right up revealing her whole leg up to the groin. The boy stares for a long time at her pretty, rounded thighs in their smooth casing of silk and

ARCIBALDO DE LA CRUZ

with their spattering of blood. This image is indelibly stamped on his memory; and when he grows up and becomes a famous potter, his erotic urges become associated with an imperative compulsion to kill. Moreover, when he cuts himself while shaving, the sight of blood immediately conjures up the memory of the maid's legs in his mind. But he is a victim of "Sod's Law": every time he is about to do away with a woman, the victim he has picked out with darting, lustful eyes is either killed by someone else or dies accidentally. His crimes elude his grasp—which of course means, symbolically, that it is love which is eluding him. In other words, Arcibaldo is impotent; he is incapable of putting his desires into effect, nor can he, as a preliminary measure, break free from the shackles they create. (The symbolism of the story implies these two aspects: killing = making love, possessing; and killing = neutralising oppressive forces. With his musical box, Arcibaldo casts spells on the maid, on a nun, and then on a girl of good family.)

As he is unable to make use of his virility, and is cheated of his prey the very moment he thinks it is in his grasp, he is forced to find compensations in his imagination, and slithers into a sadomasochistic syndrome. Like some ultra-refined aesthete, he makes his quest for impossible pleasure quite extraordinarily complicated. He spots a wax tailor's dummy in the window of a dress shop and takes it home to live with him. He invites a woman to his house, cunningly forces her to undress, and puts her clothes on to the dummy, carrying out thereby a kind of transfer he finds highly stimulating. At the same time, he feverishly prepares the woman's murder down to the tiniest detail. His idea is to do away with her in the pottery kiln. He rushes out to regulate the flames, carefully checks the temperature, comes back, fondles some women's underwear in a drawer, and carries in a tray with two glasses of brandy on it that he has filled before her arrival (he has put only water in his own glass, in order to keep a clear head!). He kisses the dummy on the mouth, then the woman on the cheek, and is just about to experience a marvellous pyrotechnic orgasm when his plans are ruined by a gaggle of American tourists who unexpectedly come to visit his workshop. The woman leaves with the visitors and in the end it is the dummy he consigns to the flames, unable as he is, yet again, to make love except via an effigy.

He could in fact very well end up like Francisco, with his repressions disguised by the calm façade of a monastic existence (he too is a devout Christian). But he courageously makes the decision that saves him just in the nick of time: he exorcises the clinging memory of his mother and of the maid's thighs. He sticks the musical box in a bag, which he then throws in a river rather in the same way as one drowns kittens. The mechanical ballerina floats for a moment on the surface of the water, then slowly sinks. Arcibaldo is cured. He sees a grasshopper (or is it a praying mantis?) at the foot of a tree. He could easily squash it with the tip of his walking stick. But he decides not to, and throws away his stick. A new man, he strides away under the trees and takes the arm of a woman who has come to meet him.

The Style

The composition of Buñuel's films, with their almost mischievously intelligent mastery of style, has consistently discouraged the efforts of those critics who find it impossible to unravel their precise structural patterns. Maurice Blanchot has some relevant remarks to make in this connection: "The word composition always irritates me, and reminds me of the way Goethe answered back at Eckermann: 'What a nasty word composition is. We have the French to thank for it, and we ought to get rid of it as quickly as we can. How could it be said, for instance, that Mozart "composed" *Don Giovanni?*' "[22] Similarly, one has to admit that Buñuel did not "compose" *L'Age d'Or, The Exterminating Angel, Simon of the Desert* or any other of his masterpieces. For he has an innate sense of what is or is not poetic licence. As a director, he has never allowed himself to be governed by the "rules" which are supposed to underlie the grouping of images, the ordering of sequences, and the dovetailing of the editing, according to those cinematic rhetoricians-cum-carpenters who see themselves as teachers but are themselves incapable of planing a plank or knocking in a nail. When Buñuel prepares a shot, he is less concerned with the camera-angle than with injecting, almost imperceptibly, a particular climate or tone into the camera's field of vision. The problems of cinematic language as such have never worried him; he prefers to follow his instinct, his mood, or his sense of improvisation when working.

The artist in him cannot be separated from the man. He walks, laughs, and has a drink with friends in just the same way as he conceives a scene, shoots it, and then fits it organically into his story-line. Maybe his only conscious struggle with himself is to reduce to a minimum anything that might be considered formally facile, to resist the temptation of special effects too flashy to be really honest, and above all to avoid the sort of gimcrack persuasiveness made possible by a musical accompaniment. With each new film, Buñuel has shown an even greater determination to strip down his style and steer clear of over-obvious dream-like effects. The end product of this process has been *Tristana*. At first sight, the casual observer might suppose that in no way did it differ stylistically from the run-of-the-mill stuff churned out by someone like Jean Delannoy. But that is the whole point: Buñuel's superiority lies not in his intensity, profundity or style, it is something intrinsic. His films obey different kinds of laws, which I myself would term dialectic. The true originality of Buñuel's cinema is that it slips into the mould of the most *cliché*-ridden type of film-making, and then destroys it by bursting out from within.

Buñuel covers his tracks by mimicking banality. He serves us with a light-hearted farrago of spontaneous invention, serious thinking, ironic winks at the audience, powerfully constructed and original creativity, and a combination of burlesque and tragedy. He slips back and forth from unselfconscious self-discipline to disciplined unselfconsciousness as airily as Picasso. In *Arcibaldo de la Cruz*—probably because Buñuel seems almost to be parodying himself—one can perceive better than in any of his other films how he manages to inject madness into realism, and how a piece of frothy entertainment can be shot through and through with black humour. He does not indulge in any cunning aesthetic devices or spectacular dream sequences, but pads unobtrusively up to his subject in order to be able to sink his teeth into it more devastatingly.

Atheism

The whole of *La Mort en ce jardin* is a veiled attack on Christianity, the church and its clergy. In it, Buñuel places the believer in such a predicament that under the pressure of his most vital, daily necessities his belief reveals itself to be an imposture. A religion that is based on the blackmail of divine grace is subjected to one of Buñuel's favourite disquisitive methods. Just as once you have removed an object's utilitarian relationship with its environment its latent reality emerges, so if you abolish social conventions and strip away the masks that are imposed on us by the comedy of human relations the characters suddenly reveal their genuine mentality. Crusoe on his island, the group of people in *Le Mort en ce jardin* who have to hack their way through virgin forest, and the bourgeois in *The Exterminating Angel* who are trapped in their drawing-room have all been forced to come face to face with themselves. They have had to drop their intellectual and moral disguises and reveal themselves nakedly for what they are. This method results, of course, in a direct attack on the very *raison d'être* of our civilisation's masquerades, and especially that of the biggest sham of all: God.

If the beginning of the story told in *La Mort en ce jardin* drags a little it is because Buñuel wants us to be perfectly acquainted with the men and women whose terrible trek through the jungle he then goes on to describe. One might very well suppose that the whole thing begins when a white cat pushes open a door and has a book flung at it by Chark. But in fact nothing either begins or ends in this film. Everything is transitory. Good is but a transitory aspect of evil, and evil a fleeting guise of good, and it is no good referring to the tenets of classical morality. What may seem to be a crime can turn out to be a good deed, and vice versa. It is a film about ambiguity.

It falls into three parts. First we are shown the lives of the

Charles Vanel (with headscarf) and Georges Marchal in LA MORT EN CE JARDIN, with a young Michel Piccoli at right

people in a diamond-prospecting village—their pleasures, their hopes and their chicanery, as well as their revolt when they receive an expulsion order from the military governor of the province. Two people in particular stand out in this not very savoury context: Chark, an athletic, courageous and down-to-earth adventurer, and Maria, a gentle deaf and dumb girl. The others—the missionary, Maria's aged father, the prostitute, the trader, the soldiers, the officers—are all, in their various ways, models of selfishness, pride, vanity and cowardice. It should be noted that the missionary proves no exception to the rule. Father Lizzardi, who goes around in a white civilian suit, gives himself the airs of an *avant-garde* priest in order to be able to inculcate, almost without seeming to do so, the message of Christ that calls for submissiveness in the oppressed: "Take care, the rebellion will result in repression . . . I'm talking to you as a friend and not as a priest

... For all they that take the sword shall perish with the sword ..." He wears a superb wristwatch ("It also tells you the date"), which was given to him as well as to all the other priests at the mission by the directors of a colonialist company ("It was a present from Northern Refineries"). Castin, the old church-going father, wants to marry Djin, the tart, and open a bistro with her in Marseille, so he can finish his days in peace and make Maria happy. He wears close to his heart a little leather purse full of the rough diamonds which will enable him to succeed in his project and keep Djin for himself alone. Chark is arrested by some soldiers. They accuse him of theft, and frogmarch him off to prison through the church in the middle of a service that is being conducted by Father Lizzardi (whose lay brother is the devout and circumspect Castin). As they pass the altar, each soldier genuflects, but Chark, whose hands are tied behind his back, does not budge. One of the soldiers forces him down on to his knees by hitting his legs with a rifle butt.

After the service, Father Lizzardi goes to see Chark in his prison cell which he is sharing, and finds a man whose gunshot wounds have not been treated by the police. "Remember your soul," says the priest to the dying wretch.

In heartfelt tones, Chark tells Lizzardi that he wants to make a confession and to send a letter to his mother. He asks for something to write with. Hardly has one of the jailers given him pen and ink when he leaps on him, viciously stabs him in the eye with the pen, throws the inkpot in the other jailer's face, shuts them in his cell and escapes. He then blows up the army's munitions dump, which sets off rioting everywhere. Martial law is declared, the army fires on the population, takes hostages and shoots them. A price is set on the heads of Chark and Castin who are believed (wrongly) to be behind the riots. Father Lizzardi is completely overwhelmed by events.

The second part of the film begins with five very different

people, who might almost have been chosen for their capacity to hate or to love each other (Chark, Castin, Lizzardi, Maria and Djin), hastily leaving a province that is being put to fire and sword. They are helped in their escape by Chenko, the trader, who takes them away in his yacht. But when the police take chase, Chenko betrays them and is killed by Chark; and the five refugees find themselves in the depths of a dangerous terrain that seethes with snakes, strident birds, thorns and insects. Their contact with physical suffering very quickly engenders a feeling of helplessness, which reduces them to the condition of an ordinary group of human beings whose only concern is survival. Their whole system of values is upset by the pressures of loneliness, hunger, rain, cold, darkness and fear. They come near to delirium. The priest mumbles prayers, or tells the story of what happened to the boiled eggs when he was at the seminary. Castin keeps on saying: "We are all guilty." Djin gives way to despondency. Maria seems to be somewhere else. Only Chark has any spunk left in him. He hacks his way through the jungle, determined to get the better of the situation by acting vigorously. Lizzardi follows his example, and veers imperceptibly from contemplation and resignation to action. He digs up roots to feed himself and his companions, gives them water to drink in his holy chalice (this time to quench their thirst and not to give them Holy Communion), and after much heart-searching decides to tear out the pages of his Bible in order to light a fire.

In so doing, Lizzardi shows that he has realised the fallacy of traditional Christian attitudes; he demonstrates that for him the struggle for the survival of those with him is much more important than praying for the salvation of their souls.

The third part of the film opens with Chark going on reconnaissance and finding the wreck of a crashed aeroplane. There are no survivors. Their luggage contains food, clothes, and jewellery. "God has saved us," cries Castin. "And fifty people had to die for

Charles Vanel and Simone Signoret in LA MORT EN CE JARDIN

him to be able to do so," retorts Chark. In a flash, the situation changes. Our five characters forget that adversity had made them friends, and revert to what they were "before" (c.f. Crusoe's and Man Friday's arrival in England). As though back in a society based on profit and a hypocritical morality, Castin's sanity gives way; one by one, he throws the diamonds into a pond as though they were pebbles, and kills first Djin, then Father Lizzardi who tries to bring him to his senses. In the end, Chark shoots him. The film finishes with Chark, the positive hero, and Maria, the innocent girl, managing to escape the forest by going down river on an inflatable dinghy. But will they survive? And for how long?

This very simply narrated story is interspersed with strikingly unusual images that lend poetry and tragedy to what seems to be no more than an adventure story. One thinks, for instance, of Maria with her hair caught in some thorns, of the snake being devoured by ants (a reminder of the bees that kill the donkey in *Las Hurdes*), the postcard on which the bustle and clamour of the Champs-Elysées suddenly comes to life, Djin in evening dress in the middle of a clearing, or the priest caught in the prostitute's bedroom and laid open to the ribald jests of those who find him there without being able to explain himself. ("Don't judge me from appearances," he says. "Difficult, isn't it?" remarks Djin, "to have people judge you when you're not guilty.")

La Mort en ce jardin is a film that makes the most thorough use of ambiguity because it is an accurate reflection of the way people hesitate, recoil from, and decide against certain acts, and then change their mind. But its fundamental meaning could not be clearer. Buñuel is once again pointing to the total pointlessness of Christian faith in adversity. Man can count only on himself in such situations; God, who is generally a cosy alibi, proves to be a useless hypothesis. Father Lizzardi is obviously the character who most interests Buñuel in *La Mort en ce jardin*. The director does not hate him because he is a priest, or because he has more or less been bribed by the financial powers that be. He simply watches him act, from the same humanist viewpoint he adopts in every film. Unlike Fellini, Bresson and Rossellini, he does not feel that it is worth wasting his time on theology; nor is he torn, like the intellectually exhibitionistic Pasolini, between Marx and Christ, or between Freud and Jakobson. On the other hand, he would be thoroughly at home making a film based on the diary of a country priest who was having difficulty in staying on the straight and narrow path of virtue, so long as his outpourings were sincere. For Buñuel, it is an incontrovertible fact that priests are men, and that in certain rare circumstances the man wearing the dog collar can act in a way which almost challenges the very vocation of a priest, such as the Carmelites (enclosed nuns) who in a famous incident left their cloister to run to the help of the wounded, such as the worker-priests, or those who wish to get married, or those who take to the hills and fight alongside the guerrilleros. And Lizzardi does precisely this sort of thing: he needs to drink in order to quench his thirst, and the chalice is a suitable vessel; he needs to make a fire in order to warm himself, and the pages of the Bible are made of paper. I do not think that Buñuel had any blasphemous intentions here. He simply wanted to illustrate the vital demands of practical morality when they contrast with those of a mystifying morality. This constructively critical approach, which sees things in humanist rather than theological perspective, becomes even subtler in *Nazarin*. Nazarin takes over where Lizzardi left off. He knows everything there is to know about starvation and poverty, both his own and other people's. As a result, he sides resolutely with the oppressed and refuses to compromise with the Pharisees, even if they are his superiors. And yet his goodness, his love and his charity keep on bobbing to the surface; and all his attempts to achieve a fraternal victory are hounded almost diabolically by failure. Like worker-priests, or all priests who are out fighting on a social or even political front, his role remains basically that of a missionary. All things considered, he is no different from someone like Billy Graham; he uses a less shockingly brash kind of approach, but is nevertheless an equal hindrance to the cause of man's freedom. His aim is proselytism, and not the definitive deliverance of the individual from the superstitions and countless spiritual obligations that are imposed on him by the Church. Nazarin, because of his faith, is blind to the fact that by siding with the victims rather than first taking up arms against their oppressors he is prolonging and reinforcing his own illusions. Nazarin's sincerity has feet of clay, and can only result in a combination of resignation and trickery. This comes home to him when he accepts the pineapple, as will be seen from the plot.

Nazarin is adapted from a novel by Benito Pérez Galdós (1843–1920), a Spanish writer who also wrote *Tristana* (which Buñuel also made into a film), and who has often been compared to Tolstoy, Balzac, Zola, and, perhaps most accurately, to Dickens minus the sentimentality. *Nazarin* was written in 1895, and belongs to Galdos's "mystical" or "evangelical" phase, which began in 1892 and was his final creative period. The novelist describes a priest, Don Nazario Zaharin, who towards the end of the Nineteenth century tries to live in as faithful a manner as possible to the Gospel. Andara, a prostitute, follows him; then they are joined by the beautiful Beatriz. He teaches them resignation, asceticism, love of their neighbour and forgiveness. As poor as the people around them, they travel from village to village in the best tradition of the picaresque novel, and answer the malice of those they meet, both the governed and the governors, with meekness and kindness. When he is struck on the right cheek, our quixotic Franciscan proffers his left cheek. They are abused, scorned, beaten up, and accused of charlatanism. When they are escorted into town, the similarity between Nazarin's Calvary and the Passion of Christ becomes increasingly striking. Nazarin is struck down with typhus; during his delirium in hospital he sees himself walking up towards Golgotha, hoping that he will be nailed to the cross; then, as he conducts Mass he meets Jesus, who speaks to him. They are the last words of the book: "You are still alive, my son. You are in my holy hospital, suffering for me. The two unfortunate women and the thief who followed your teaching are in prison. You cannot conduct Mass, I cannot be with you in flesh and blood, and this Mass is but a hallucination of your sick mind. Take some rest, you deserve it. You have done something for me. Be satisfied; I know that you will do much more."

Buñuel transfers the action from Spain to Mexico at the turn of the century, at the time when Porfirio Diaz's dictatorship was in power with the support of big landowners. His film may at first sight seem to be a faithful adaptation of Galdós's novel; but in fact, through certain changes of emphasis and the addition of a scene here and there that bear his own particular stamp, Buñuel completely changes the overall meaning and integrates the film into his personal universe. Even when he seems simply to be illustrating certain of Galdós's scenes, he always enriches them with a little touch, a detail, or a gesture that completely changes their centre of gravity. What is so striking about the poor, resourceless Nazarin is no longer his exemplary humility, his devotion to Christ, or his practical experience of faith, hope and charity, nor even his redeeming taste of suffering, but his uselessness, his masochism, and the harmful effects of his activity. The final sequence, which is open to any number of interpretations, is both the most intensely disturbing and at the same time the most revealing if one takes the trouble to see it in the context of the director's overall poetic terms of reference. Buñuel deliberately veers away from Galdós's original before Nazarin's typhus attack. He has his hero separated from his followers, imagining, most plausibly, that the Church establishment is embarrassed by the scandal he has caused and does not want to draw too much attention to him. A clergyman says to him: "By order of the diocese, which has arranged everything with the civil authorities, you will no longer be accompanied by your followers. You will be escorted separately by a man in civilian clothes. That is all they managed to obtain, but even so it'll be less humiliating. Aren't you interested in knowing how your case is progressing? You'll at least have to admit your rash and foolish acts. They are right to say that you are an anti-conformist, a rebellious character. It's going to be difficult to make you see reason and realise that your habitual behaviour is not only most unpriest-like but highly offensive to the Church that you claim to love and obey . . ."[23]

So Nazarin walks along in the heat of the sun with his guardian. An unknown woman comes up to him and offers him a pineapple. At first he refuses it; but when he remembers that this is not a gift to a priest, as the woman cannot possibly know that he is one,

The compassionate dwarf in NAZARIN

he accepts it. Meanwhile, in the background, we can hear the deafening roll of the drums of Calanda.

During the twenty-four hours of Good Friday, from midday to the following midday, all the inhabitants of the Spanish town of Calanda come out into the streets and madly beat drums of all sizes until they are exhausted and their hands are bloody. While still a very small boy, Buñuel was deeply struck by this obsessive din that accompanies the agony of Christ. In 1964, he thought of making a medium-length film about this event and about the celebration of Holy Week in his native village. But he gave up the project. In 1966, his son, Juan-Luis Buñuel made a short film in Calanda which concentrated on the people who, alone or in groups, persist in drumming all through the night as though exorcising

Nazarin steps out through the fields

demons. His film won the Grand Prix at the Tours Festival in 1967.

The drums of Calanda can be heard in *L'Age d'Or*, where they emphasise certain sequences, and in particular those where Modot gives free rein to his bottled-up desires; their use in *Nazarin* has a similar purpose.

Nazarin, which Buñuel made in Mexico in 1958 immediately after two French productions (*La Mort en ce jardin* and *Cela s'appelle l'aurore*), and just before *La Fièvre monte à El Pao*, was widely underestimated and misunderstood. At the time, for those who were unable to draw the vital parallels with *L'Age d'Or*, its deeper significance seemed difficult to decipher. Its thematic ambiguity even resulted in contradictory interpretations: the representatives of the Office Catholique International du Cinéma were thinking of awarding their prize to it at the 1959 Cannes Film Festival, while militant atheists described the film as a masterpiece of blasphemy.

This temporary atmosphere of ambiguity vanished when people saw what Buñuel went on to make (in particular *Viridiana, Simon of the Desert* and *La Voie lactée,* all of which develop the themes of *Nazarin* with a verve reminiscent of the stark, explosive violence of *L'Age d'Or*).

Nazarin is an extraordinary rich and complex film. It moves forward by continually turning situations upside down. It is thought-provoking not because it works out a thesis but because it uses poetry to pose fundamental questions about our condition. Buñuel condemns all metaphysical hypocrisy and demands that man be recognised by man. This recognition can only genuinely occur when all types of hypothetical recourse to a transcendental order have been ruled out. The parable contained in *Nazarin* combines the passion of a man who is tempted by saintliness with variations on the theme of the misfortunes of virtue. The allusion to Sade is quite explicit in the superb scene where the plague-stricken woman refuses the priest's help and calls for her lover:

Don Nazario: Remember that this life is but a highway. Bear with your suffering and prepare your soul for the joy of seeing yourself in God's presence.
Lucia: I just want to see Juan.
Don Nazario: Forget the passions of this world, my daughter. The Lord is giving you time to examine your conscience. Think of the heaven that awaits you.
Lucia: Juan!
Don Nazario: I'm speaking to you as a priest and I assure you that you can still save yourself. You only need repent your sins.
Lucia: Juan![24]

This priest of the poor is utterly devoted to his ministry, and sincerely wants to live out the lessons of Christ. But at the same time he has trouble in coping with the demands of practical morality and those of a religious code of conduct. On one side, the Church frowns on his activity, and on the other he feels cut off from society. Although his actions spring from the noblest and most genuine motives, they always result in disaster for him and for others. He prays for the life of a sick child, and the child recovers. So he is taken to be a miracle-worker and is asked to continue his performance, thus fanning the flames of superstition. He accepts the presence of Beatriz and Andara because he wants them to live in communion with God. But he soon realises that they have followed him not because they want to get closer to God, but because, subconsciously, they want to obtain the love of a flesh-and-blood human being rather than the ethereal kindness of one of God's messengers. He lives off alms, and asks a grasping head-foreman if he can have a piece of bread in return for working; in so doing, he replaces workers who are on strike and becomes, in effect, a blackleg. Most of the scenes demonstrate how failure inevitably attends all behaviour based on the principles of Christianity, an ethos that destroys man in order better to be able to save him, and saves him temporarily in order better to destroy him again, here on earth, and save him even more thoroughly in paradise. It is an ethos that humbles man and exalts him according to the whim of circumstance, that hoodwinks and lauds him by constantly ramming the image of Christ down his throat. This Christ is a Protean figure, alternately elusive and close, imperceptible and intrusive, fraternal and distant, tyrannical and obliging, accusing and defending—all because of his double nature, a quality enlarged upon with great relish by Monsieur Richard, the distinguished-looking head waiter of the posh Tours restaurant in *La Voie lactée*. Nazarin is in the thrall of the New Testament just as Don Quixote is totally guided by the canons of chivalry; he is unable to reconcile within himself his aspirations as a man and his Christ-like exaltation. He is torn between the human and the divine.

At the end of the story of Nazarin, we realise that Buñuel has been developing his criticism on two levels: first, he completely debunks the contradictions of the common attitude of arrogant humility by demonstrating that Christian charity is ineffectual; secondly, he uses the example of the ingenuous Nazarin to expose the repugnant Pharisaism of a complacent Christian establishment that gives all the help it can to landlords, judges and colonels. When the story ends (and there has been no musical accompaniment up to then), the rolling drums that can be heard as Nazarin receives the pineapple bring home to us the utter collapse of all his illusions: suddenly, he seems to spring back to real life as he discovers his primordial loneliness—and his freedom. The whole film's narrative and poetic strands converge towards this limpidly beautiful image. One feels that from this moment on Nazarin's unsheathed conscience is going to draw from within him the strength he needs for his salvation, rather than begging it from On High.

The critics, who always start quibbling about the form of Buñuel's films when the content proves too much for them, often dismiss his moral message as simplistic, limited and crude. They condescendingly slate his films in the name of the admiration they feel towards the director of *L'Age d'Or* (while pretending to forget they hate *L'Age d'Or* as well).

Buñuel's message may be limited; but I fail to see why it should be any broader or more complicated. It is brutally succinct, calling a spade a spade, and dividing our society into two categories—the baddies and those who are not baddies. Action and passivity are the result of a choice that totally commits a man and has less to do with morals than with politics. In other words, there is the Right and there is the Left. This simplification must necessarily seem frightfully vulgar to those well brought-up people who would never dream of kicking a blind man, give money to good causes, raise their hats to passing hearses, and listen, with concern written all over their faces, to a poor man's hard luck story while keeping an attentive eye on his niece's breasts. These are the same people who feel shocked at the accounts they read in their newspapers of massacres or of apartheid, and who are moved when they hear military music or see a dignitary of the Church blessing some weapons. One probably has to be left-wing in order to understand the blazing truth of this necessary simplification. The French philosopher, Alain, said in 1930 that anyone who tells you that the words "left-wing" and "right-wing" are meaningless is bound not to be a man of the Left. When faced with Buñuel's films, the conscious or unconscious champions of the Right comfort themselves by putting on a rather disgusted air and talking of his "obsessions."

Buñuel is a left-wing film-maker. A quarter of a century after the end of the Second World War, the Left of the western world is weary, disillusioned, divided, megalomaniac, and tortured, and has become bourgeoisified and bureaucratic. It could, I think, learn a lot from Buñuel's attitudes, his hatred for authority and its attendant priests, policemen and soldiers, his rehabilitation of *amour fou,* and his advocacy of a return to revolutionary fervour.

All Buñuel's works contain, by implication, the warning against the Utopia of reformism that is to be found in *La Fièvre monte à El Pao.*

"It's like many other films I've made," is Buñuel's comment on the film (which was Gérard Philipe's last appearance on the screen). What Buñuel was implying by that understated remark was that it was made under a commercial set-up and that he probably did not have quite as free a hand as he would have liked. The film does indeed have serious faults. After a short introductory sequence whose documentary virulence is reminiscent of *Las Hurdes,* there is a flurry of purely anecdotal twists and turns. When

Inès, a widow with a black veil over her face, comes to see Governor Gual, he pounces on her and rips open her bodice—a vintage piece of Buñuel. But it is only one of many such isolated good moments in a narrative that often drags terribly.

There is no sinew in the construction of the film, and inspiration more than once seems to be lacking. The characters are always signing documents or picking up the telephone for no apparent reason; one would like to see them involved in a nexus of more visually conceived contradictions. This overall flaw becomes particularly irritating towards the end: the whole meaning of the film is put across by one sentence of the commentary which has obviously been tacked on in the last resort to make up for the ambiguity of the narrative itself.

It would however be a great mistake to suppose that *La Fièvre monte à El Pao* is just a standard adventure film concocted from a mixture of exoticism and conventional psychology. Yet again Buñuel shows an absolutely uncompromising attitude when it comes down to basic essentials, and one realises that a minor film by Buñuel is always worth more than a so-called major work by Bresson or Pasolini. *La Fièvre monte à El Pao* is an unquestionably honest political film about Fascism and its accomplices.

It is set in an imaginary South American country, with a dictatorship of wealthy landowners over a *Lumpenproletariat*. The Church is right behind the State. Union leaders and other opponents of the regime (the intellectuals, in particular) are behind bars. Opposite the governor's luxurious villa looms a sinister-looking prison. The "political" prisoners are treated like common criminals and work in irons.

We then see the governor in a fit of jealousy, slapping his wife who has just been unfaithful to him, then putting his white uniform back in place and striding out of his drawing-room on to a terrace where he makes a patriotic speech to the crowds in honour of the country's national holiday. Behind him, seated on a dais, an impressive selection of Church and army dignitaries listen to him, then pompously applaud him. His high-flown speech is particularly unconvincing because we have just seen him behaving in such a childishly petulant way with his wife.

During the speech, a rebel who has been hiding in a barn shoots the governor. The patriotic festivities, which have begun in an atmosphere of enthusiasm thanks to a well-timed distribution of free meat, end in chaos. And the days that follow are marked by intrigues in the palace and the parliament for the appointment of an interim successor, arbitrary arrests, summary judgements, wrangling and blackmail. The police, who are stupid and unreasoning by definition, carry out the orders of the civil servants with all the efficiency of the SS. The man who holds the reins of power during this troubled period is Ramon Vasquez, an ambitious, idealistic under-secretary. He seizes this opportunity to reinforce one or two clauses of a forgotten law and tries to improve the prisoners' lot. He insists that they no longer be deprived of their statutory rest period, and has the irons taken off the political prisoners. But he is not any the less ambitious for being idealistic. He seduces the governor's widow in order to satisfy a thirst for power that is hardly, if at all, tempered by his sense of justice. He revels in his own happiness. He has managed to "humanise" the repression.

But a permanent new governor is appointed. He honours the prison with an official visit and brings Ramon back to reality with a bump. "What are these men doing?" he asks, pointing at the convicts. "They're resting," Ramon answers. "I want them to get back to work immediately," retorts the governor, "because when they rest they start thinking, and that's dangerous."

Ramon is perfectly aware of the double game he is forced to play by his position in a system that he has agreed to serve. He realises that both politically and socially the *régime* is detestable. But he tries to improve it rather than fight it, in the very best tradition of Christians and sentimental socialists. He wants to be a just man, in Camus's sense of the word. Like Nazarin, he prefers an absolute purity of attitude and of emotions to the ambivalence of a fully conscious act which, in the case of the wandering priest for instance, would consist of staying on the building site, taking part in the class struggle and standing up to the foreman rather than going off and plucking a twig through lack of interest in a reality that does not fit in with his saintly designs. Ramon refuses to get his hands dirty by answering conservative violence with a violence that liberates. He persists in flying in the face of the evidence and thinking that the origins of oppression lie in an inevitable flaw in the institutions (which are imperfect because they are human, as Christ would have said), whereas in fact they result from an inhuman concentration of means of production. If he dared rip away the deceptive labels ("evil," "injustice," "egoism," "the Devil"), he would find that they concealed more concrete scourges, such as banks, stock exchanges, barracks, United Fruit, Union Minière, Raffineries du Nord, or wealthy traders (like a certain Praxédès Mateo who offers Simon of the Desert a new, and higher, column).

Ramon Vasquez is a kind of lay saint, who believes passionately in lenient and charitable behaviour, but who fails to see that his position is untenable: it is impossible to be a just man in a world where the most everyday gesture and the most trifling thought are perverted by a system based on the profit motive. Ramon Vasquez sees as a disgrace what is simply a rigged interplay of capital appreciation and constitutional liberties. He indulges in a bit of breast-beating: "The rest of our lives will not suffice for us to get ourselves pardoned!" This fallacious sense of guilt instils an even fiercer desire in him to defend his ideal; but not for a moment does he think of putting his ideal to the test with a few facts, which would enable him to realise that he was using it as an alibi. His upright attitude, his wishy-washy accusations, his hinted condemnations and his silent way of seeing that as little damage as

Gérard Philipe and María Felix in LA FIEVRE MONTE A EL PAO

possible is done are simply unconscious grist to the government's mill: they adore his abortive courage, his abstract sense of rebellion, and his attachment to the mirage of an inner life—all things which make the obscenities of dividends and of police and military legislation look morally respectable. The president of the Republic sings the praises of the young man. Ramon is decorated and becomes the pride of the country—a kind of Dr. Schweitzer. He is well on the road towards a Nobel Peace Prize.

At the end Ramon realises how blind he has been; he sees himself as a traitor. He tears up a decree that is going to destroy people's liberty—an act that is bound to result in his being removed from office and sentenced to death. The commentary concludes: "This categorical refusal is the harbinger of his own death and the sign that he is a free man. Ramon Vasquez has fulfilled his destiny." This last-minute salvation obviously does not convince either the spectator or for that matter the character. Inès has previously hinted that pulling this sort of rabbit out of a hat is not enough: "One second of courage is not enough to redeem years of cowardice." This is Buñuel's lucidly political answer to all those who (to the delight of those in power) talk cleverly about the relationship between collaborationism and the metaphysics of redemption. It has a remarkable power to ungild the pill that film-makers like Bresson and Rossellini would have us swallow. And more specifically it unmasks, by implication, the abject way in which a film like *Il Generale della Rovere* dishonestly glosses over and justifies the conduct of its hero.

Reflecting as it did the state of affairs in several South American, Middle Eastern and African countries, the imaginary dictatorship under which Ramon Vasquez lives was extraordinarily topical in 1960; it still is today. The police methods of El Pao are exactly those which were enforced by Gaullist France in Algeria. A rebel is captured and coolly murdered (like the gamekeeper's son in *L'Age d'Or*) by the two soldiers who are bringing him back to the town in a jeep and who tell him to get out and stretch his legs; later they talk of an attempted escape. This was the device that in Algeria became notorious under the name of *"corvée de bois"* (woodgathering party). This sort of thing has been continuing ever since the film was made, and not just in Vietnam; and political prisoners still fill prisons, detention centres and psychiatric hospitals. And the Ramon Vasquez of this world are still concerned about them and still sign petitions demanding their freedom.

But above all Buñuel is painting a picture of Franco's Spain. His parable shows that it is not possible to reform a dictatorial *régime* from within, and purely through intellectual force of argument; one has to have the courage to overthrow it by force first by organising rebellious action (from union militancy to the constitution of a revolutionary militia), to sow the seeds of defeatism in the army, and encourage desertion, or else to leave the country and undertake a campaign from outside aimed at undermining its authority and its good name. From his exile in Mexico, Buñuel was giving us his thoughts on the whole problem of ends and means. *La Fièvre monte à El Pao* is a great Spanish film of considerable international relevance that most critics dismissed just a little too hastily. *Cahiers du Cinéma* (No. 104, February 1960), for instance, said of it: "Buñuel has been too respectful towards the intentions of his second-rate subject—a prisoners' uprising on a South American island and the attitudes of various governments towards it—and has forgotten to direct his actors." The writer of the same article nevertheless described Buñuel not only as a genius but as a great technician, which is a naïve or sly way of casting aspersions on his genius: "Figueroa's photography is dreadfully amateurish. But we should not forget that in *Nazarin* Buñuel showed that he had become a technician, and also one of the greatest technicians of all time." Few and far between were the perspicacious critics who devoted to *La Fièvre monte à El Pao* the sympathetic attention it deserved. One of these was Raymond Borde in particular, who managed to point to an aspect of it which, I think, escaped all other critics: "*La Fièvre monte à El Pao* has a farcical side to it that contains some excellent political sacrilege. The serious-looking tyrants are always trying to get the better of each other. Gual has a go at Vasquez, and just as he is about to get rid of him he is himself executed. Vasquez steps straight into his boots, but gets involved in a government plot. The president eases out his own brother, and so on. The only constants in this merry-go-round are two symbolic policemen, who imperturbably obey whoever happens to be in power. And everything happens as though some grotesque collection of puppets were playing at being governors, presidents and ministers. The mechanics of the system are stripped open to the light of day, and as a result nothing can withstand the winds of satire. What can there be behind the haughtiness of officials, behind the demagogy ("I was myself a simple worker," simpers President Barreiro), or behind the uniforms? Nothing but a startling political vacuum and a load of nasty ham actors who end up by believing in their own characters."

Love the Redeemer

Doctor Valerio, in *Cela s'appelle l'aurore*, is on the other hand a positive and exemplary hero. This film is a remarkable adaptation by Buñuel of a fine novel by Emmanuel Roblès, who took the title from the last line of Giraudoux's play *Electre:*

> Narsès: What do you call it, when the day breaks, like today, and when everything has been spoilt, when everything has been pillaged, and when even so the air can be breathed, and when one has lost everything, when the city burns, when innocent people kill each other, but when the guilty are in their death throes, in some corner of the daybreak?
>
> The Beggar: It has a very beautiful name, Narsès. It is called the dawn.

Through the mouthpiece of Doctor Valerio, Buñuel once again advocates subversion and makes statements that are very rarely to be heard in the cinema, and almost never in the French cinema. He says that in Western contemporary society the honour of the individual no longer coincides with the duties of the citizen, that the moral system is just as cankered as the social system, that the police are the concrete manifestation of this whole system, and that under no circumstances should one come to terms with the institutions that control this society from top to bottom. In other words, one should totally reject all taboos and all laws, and feel at all times and in all circumstances in a state of insurrection. One's self-respect, therefore, requires one to give refuge in one's home to the worker who has just murdered his boss, and never to shake hands with a policeman.

On some Mediterranean island, a rich industrialist and landowner ruthlessly exploits his employees. He is not interested in doing anything about the disgraceful working conditions that operate in his factory, where one worker has just lost some fingers in a dangerous and unprotected machine. A farm-hand whose wife is seriously ill is evicted by him from his hovel. This industrialist is an energetic and respected man who is on excellent terms with the priest, recognises his wife's qualities and is greatly attached to his son, who will later step into his shoes and whom he wants to bring up in his own image. But like any self-respecting bourgeois head of a family, he bolsters up his virility once in a while by inviting some of his younger female employees into his bed; and when there is no bed to hand, he simply uses his desk.

The peace and quiet of this little town is a clever disguise for the injustices of capitalism. Cats stretch themselves in the sun, the children play cowboys and Indians or mime an execution, dirty old men rape little girls, and both the police superintendent and Doctor Valerio go about their business (their two jobs stand at opposite poles in this compelling story).

The police superintendent has artistic, even *avant-garde* tastes. A Dali-like Christ hangs on the wall of his office; and he knows whole speeches from Claudel's plays off by heart, and his complete works, in the compact one-volume Pléiade edition, can be seen on his desk underneath a pair of handcuffs. So refined is he that he spends some time wondering which pair of gloves to take from a drawer before going out. It is not beyond him to call his underlings to heel when he sees them beating up a poor fellow in the corridors of the police station; but when he is forced by circumstances he becomes just as brutal as any of his policemen: with a sharp blow of his heel he crushes the hand of the grandfather who has sexually assaulted a little girl and has been shut up in a hen coop by the members of the family.

The doctor, on the other hand, is fully aware of the rottenness of this over-hierarchical and disgracefully unjust conservative corner of the world. He is on the side of such exploited workers as Sandro, whom he knew during the war. Sandro is a servant who is sacked and replaced by a poor peasant who comes up from the south with his whole family. At first Sandro has it in for his fellow worker, who is even needier than he is, before realising that he ought to be getting rid of the landlord instead—and, through him, the whole system that not only allows but encourages such a personification of arrogance to become rich. Unlike Ramon Vasquez in

Georges Marchal (kneeling) in CELA S'APPELLE L'AURORE

La Fièvre monte à El Pao, who is always beating about the bush and justifying himself, Valerio immediately takes up a clearcut position. He dresses people's wounds, but does not fall victim to idealism. When events require him to, he reacts in a healthy, noble way, without trying to wriggle out of his commitments. His wife misses the gay society life she led in Nice as a young girl; she is bored, and cannot understand how her husband gets genuine satisfaction out of looking after the poor in such an out-of-the-way place when he could be carving out a fine career for himself, milking rich patients on the continent. When he starts trying to explain to her why he wants to remain faithful to the role he has chosen for himself, she answers "I don't want to be just, but happy." She goes on holiday.

After his wife's departure, Valerio meets a beautiful woman called Clara, who not only admires him but understands him. They fall in love almost at first sight. The minute he has a free moment he meets her; they spend their nights together.

Sandro is evicted by the industrialist in spite of the support he gets from the doctor. He has to move temporarily to a friend's house. With a cart piled high with his pathetic furniture and his wife lying on an improvised stretcher, he makes his way through the town at festival time. This journey and this humiliation is too much for his wife, and she dies. Sandro immediately decides to avenge her death. On the day of her funeral he is not to be seen following the procession. The industrialist is having a party that evening at his villa. Sandro slips into the park, and from the terrace of the house he watches the elegant members of high society simpering as they nibble their *canapés* and sip their whiskies. He picks up a kitten and pushes open the door. There is a hush of shocked amazement. The industrialist's male secretary asks him to leave. The priest gives him a paternal lecture. But he does not listen—he just walks forward along the carpet to within a foot or two of his former boss and empties his pistol into his stomach. In the general confusion that ensues, he manages to escape. This beautifully simple and violent scene is almost like a continuation of the party sequence in *L'Age d'Or*—one of the workers has got off the cart and shot the most repulsive of the Majorcans!

Sandro seeks asylum with the doctor, who agrees to hide him in his house. His wife returns from her holiday, accompanied by her father. They hope to persuade Valerio to leave the island. A nice little nest-egg is waiting for him in Nice, where he will be able to open a practice. But very soon they discover that the murderer the police are looking for has taken refuge beneath their roof. The father-in-law flies into a temper, insults the doctor, and declares that his daughter can no longer share the life of a man who is not on the side of the police but of common criminals. They return to Nice. Clara assures Valerio that he has done the right thing. The police search the doctor's house, but find no one. Sandro has escaped through a window. A chase ensues, which is followed with interest by the inhabitants. Valerio and Clara also come out into the streets. When Sandro is finally cornered in a cul-de-sac, Valerio asks for permission to go and talk to him. He does so, but Sandro commits suicide. The doctor leans over him and kisses him. The police superintendent mumbles a few excuses and offers to shake hands with Valerio, who refuses. We next see Valerio walking along the sea front with Clara. They kiss. Three of Sandro's friends are also walking silently with them. Valerio has achieved both love and friendship. This last shot of the film has a wonderful poignancy about it.

Raymond Borde has had some very intelligent things to say about this admirable film: "I have only one reservation. Once the tragic events the film describes are over, there is bound to be an element of condescension on the part of the doctor towards the workers, whose own attitude will equally inevitably be one of affectionate humility. I feel the film ends one hour too early. The question of what happens 'afterwards' is not satisfactorily worked out. I have an uneasy feeling that Valerio's mistress may become a kind of lay patroness and that Valerio himself may end up by showing the true colours of his class. Buñuel's confidence in love as a magic solution to all conflicts amounts almost to a faith. I cannot help wondering whether this is not too lyrical an ethos to hold where social questions are concerned."[25] This criticism of Borde's is relevant because it attempts to come to terms with the problem of how to prevent an exalting, aggressive inspiration from flagging, but it is unfair because it expects more from the film than it actually sets out to achieve. And what it does achieve is enormous. It is basically a work of criticism: Doctor Valerio's negative attitude towards the Establishment does not result in the positivity of blithe optimism. Buñuel simply points the way to refusal—a refusal that leads to revolt and maybe to revolution—and he prefers to see magic powers in love rather than in revolutionary possibilities (as any orthodox Marxist-Leninist film would have done). Once again he shows that for the truly free man no achievement in politics or love is *permanent*. The final shot of *Cela s'appelle l'aurore* is only superficially a happy one: what happens after it will require further courage and further efforts.

The punch of the film is such that when first released it flummoxed the film reviewers of the French bourgeois press. ". . . an utterly silly story from start to finish that is a combination of heavy-handed social melodrama and commonplace sentiments," wrote Jean Dutourd (somebody should ask him how many melodramas he can name offhand where the central character coolly and categorically refuses to collaborate with the police). The poor fellow then goes on to admit that the film baffles him: "I should be interested to know what in fact is called 'the dawn.' There is certainly no indication of it in the film." Claude Mauriac did not appreciate its "facile anticlericalism: a priest-about-town who rubs shoulders with the party-loving rich and connives with a despicable employer"; then he tries to find fault with the film by ad-

Lucia Bosé and Georges Marchal in CELA S'APPELLE L'AURORE

ducing such ludicrous criteria of realism as the following: "this film is dishonest because the wheels of the carriages turn the wrong way. (...) It is for instance quite inconceivable that the doctor, who is the only one on the island and, on top of that, is depicted as being particularly conscientious, would sleep away from home every night without leaving an address, even if it were to make love to the beautiful Lucia Bosé." And so on and so on. His whole article revolves around details of this sort. Now let's have a look at what was written by the deeply Catholic Eric Rohmer, the future director of *Ma Nuit chez Maud,* which so delighted the French bourgeoisie, from the extreme Right to the extreme Left: "All that remains of Breton's myth of *amour fou* is something which could be found in a women's magazine serial; the aggressivity of the Twenties has become the cockiness of boarding-school inmates out on a spree. It is enough to turn anyone into a religious bigot, a policeman and a Fascist before you could say Jack Robinson! The film is just one *cliché* after another, a huge ado about nothing. I hope that Buñuel has not said his last word. For the time being anyway, he only occupies a small niche in the history of the cinema, as Dali's collaborator on *Un Chien Andalou* and *L'Age d'Or* and as Mexico's virtually only director: all in all, a pretty small niche."

Such summary dismissals of an excellent film by one of the greatest living film-makers should be considered a good sign: right-wing irritation is sure proof that this pamphleteering film has hit its target. And as in all Buñuel's films, love is still *amour fou*. But here it is more serene, more worldly and more constructive. It contrasts strongly with the wild, unbridled passion that was the hallmark of *Cumbres Borrascosas*, which Buñuel made back in 1953.

The latter film is not one which is particularly close to Buñuel's heart. "Bad casting and an over-use of Wagner's music still make me blush . . . except for the last three reels," he wrote in a letter to me dated August 26, 1960. This adaptation of Emily Brontë's novel, *Wuthering Heights,* was originally a project that Buñuel and Pierre Unik had after working on *Las Hurdes* together. The story is transposed into a Spanish setting. Buñuel creates a desolate poetic atmosphere which, for all its superficial differences, comes much closer to the spirit of the novel than did Hecht and Wyler's occasionally sentimental 1939 version. Buñuel demonstrates a natural affinity with his subject and lends it a realistic visual violence that borders on the fantastic: a toad is thrown into a fire, Eduardo pins butterflies on to a board, a pig is prepared for slaughter at the farm and knives are sharpened, Ricardo gives a fly to a spider, muslin curtains billow in the wind, and steam left by someone's breath on a window-pane gives rise to jealousy. Alexandro comes back to see Catarina, who dies in his arms. He gives vent to his grief by screaming into a gale amid swirls of dust and dead leaves. During the night, he goes to the graveyard and breaks the padlock of the burial vault with an iron bar. He goes down the steps, opens the coffin and kisses the corpse passionately. He turns round and thinks he can see Catarina, dressed in a white dress, smiling and beckoning to him—but this vision vanishes and is replaced by Ricardo, who promptly shoots him. The two dead lovers remain folded in each other's arms as Ricardo closes the burial vault.

The formal beauty of this staggering finale is reminiscent of Epstein's *La Chute de la Maison Usher* and Dreyer's *Vampyr;* but Buñuel adds a sublime and tender cruelty, and a strong human touch that both those academic classes lack. *Cumbres Borrascosas* is an overwhelming poem and a bloody, vertiginous maelstrom of romanticised *amour fou*.

It is the outcome of a process, whereas, as I have already suggested, the passion of *Cela s'appelle l'aurore* develops within the framework of a destructo-constructive humanism that is in constant danger of being hamstrung by religious, political and social myths and taboos. It is a brand of humanism that enables individuals to get rid of their complexes in a manner that encourages socialism —making the Church less sacred and the flesh more so. This humanism gets stronger and more clear-cut with Buñuel's every film, and in particular from *Robinson Crusoe* onwards. It is through love that Valerio and Clara become able to confront an unjust social system, and perhaps to destroy it with the help of the people. It is through love that Miller, the gamekeeper of *The Young One*, first feels the urges of his own sensibility, and understands that racialism is but an arrogant *façade* for his evasive conduct *vis-à-vis* himself. Love is constantly shown as something that clashes radically with bourgeois, Christian and capitalist society. Consequently, in that sort of context, love is always a question of rebellion, scandal and sin—a transcendental quality which eats away the values that have been carefully nurtured in the greenhouses of religion and state. The lawmaker sees it as a crime, adultery in Valerio's case and seduction of a minor in Miller's; but these "crimes" are the upshot of a moral attitude that has freed itself from the fetters of manicheism.

Ewie and Her Shoes

The action of *The Young One* takes place on an island somewhere off the southern coast of the United States that attracts hunters during the duck-shooting season. In a month's time, work will begin on the construction of a hunting lodge. Meanwhile, on the mainland, we hear someone scream "rape," and see a Negro leaping into a motor-boat. He takes refuge on the island, which is inhabited by three people: Pee-Wee, Ewie his nymphette-like daughter (she is thirteen or fourteen), and, in a nearby shack, Miller the gamekeeper. Pee-Wee dies. Ewie does not seem to be terribly affected by this event. Everything is simple for her: she puts shoes on the dead man's feet and eats a slice of bread and butter. The air is vibrant with sunshine and insects. Her innocence creates an atmosphere of calm and restfulness around her. She goes smilingly about her tasks with a youthful grace that scarcely suggests the adolescent which lies within her girlish body. She squashes a spider and looks after the bees—a charming, fresh figure amid her hives and her flowers. The Negro sees her and asks her to give him a can of petrol for his boat. She takes him into her house with quite disarming unselfconsciousness, takes a shower, and dries herself in front of him. Then she gives him the petrol which he pays for with a bank-note.

Miller returns from the mainland with supplies. He tells Ewie that the orphanage does not accept children over twelve. She tells him about the Negro's visit. Miller springs to his feet, grabs a gun and goes off to look for him. He spots his prey, and a chase ensues; but the Negro escapes by running off towards the swamps. Miller smashes the fugitive's hut with his rifle butt and goes back to Ewie. He undoes some of the packets, and offers the girl a dress. She tries it on, under his personal, and intentionally close, supervision. He warns her: "Be careful, not all men are like me." He does her hair, puts outsize high-heeled shoes on her feet, and asks her to take a few steps. (Chark, in *La Mort en ce jardin,* first noticed the deaf-mute girl, Maria, when she was trying on the shoes her father had bought her.) He kisses her; but then the sight of the bank-note makes him suddenly jealous, and he assails her with questions like a lover who thinks he has been betrayed: "And what did you give him in return?"

Miller and the Negro meet on the edge of the woods and have a slanging match: "I've seen plenty of filthy niggers." "You're just a white sonuvabitch. Even when I was in the army they called me nigger." Ewie finds all this very funny. In the end, Miller offers to take on the Negro as a servant. He is to live in Pee-Wee's shack. "Ewie, you'll sleep at my place tonight," he says.

That evening, the Negro plays the clarinet. Ewie beats time, then goes to bed and falls asleep. Miller turns out the light, draws the curtains, goes up to her and whispers: "Don't be afraid . . ." Next morning, wearing his best boots and with his hand on his gun, he contentedly watches the girl by a stream. "You're a woman," he says proudly. "I'll give you a chromium-plated pistol and nylon stockings."

A few hours later, a priest and his ferryman, a brute of a man called Jackson, come ashore. Miller learns that the Negro is suspected of having raped a white woman. Although he himself has just sexually initiated a girl who is well under age, he suddenly changes into a fearless and blameless meter-out of justice. He and Jackson decide to go on a punitive expedition in search of the "nigger." "I want him alive," says Jackson. Miller is less scrupulous: "If I clap eyes on him I'm going to shoot." During the evening, the priest discovers to his amazement that Ewie has not been baptised. He promises himself he will make good this lack first thing in the morning. Then he is invited to sleep in Pee-Wee's shack; when he is told that he is being given a bed that was slept in the previous night by a Negro, he has the mattress turned over! He is a good man: he is concerned with men's souls, and says that he is anti-

"Would a white woman lie, boy?" Racialism in THE YOUNG ONE

racialist; but he has clear-cut ideas about the smell of Negroes. He is a perfect example of embryonic racialism—the commonest, most underhand, and most poisonous brand of racialism. It reminds me of the people who say: "I'm firmly antiracialist, like you, but I can't help wondering how you'd react if your daughter told you she was going to marry a Negro . . ."

Miller, meanwhile, impresses on Ewie that she must say nothing of their relationship if she is asked about it by the priest.

At dawn, the priest takes Ewie down to the river in order to baptise her. He tells her that she is about to receive an incomparable gift, "a golden key that will open the gates of Paradise." After being submerged by him in the water, the girl reacts in a manner reminiscent of Man Friday after he has been given his religious talking-to by Robinson Crusoe: she looks at the priest and says: "Well? What about the golden key?" Because of Ewie's hilarious reaction to baptism, this scene has always shocked practising Protestants and Catholics—who, we may be sure, would have accepted it without a blink if, instead, the baptised girl had displayed the stupid bliss of an imbecile like Maria Goretti or of a schizo like Thérèse Martin of Lisieux, or the hysteria of the instant converted that round off so beautifully any American-style religious festival, whose excesses have been so forcefully exposed in such films as Richard Brooks's *Elmer Gantry* and Peter Watkins's *Privilege*.

Miller and Jackson capture the Negro, who explains the circumstances of the rape of which he is accused and through his sincere manner gives the impression of being innocent. They tie him to a stake; but Ewie secretly sets him free. The priest indulges in a subtle piece of blackmail. Knowing now as he does that Miller has taken advantage of Ewie he is willing not to breathe a word on condition the Negro is set free and their marriage celebrated. Then he prepares to leave with Jackson and the girl. (When I say that Miller "took advantage" of Ewie, I am using the sort of language that comes naturally to the priest; in fact, Ewie fully consented to make love, and as a result the film does not, as most commentators have suggested, centre on a rape but on an act of love.)

On his way to the boat, Jackson meets the Negro. They fight with knives. The Negro gets the better of Jackson and is in a position to slit his throat. "Go on, kill me," yells Jackson. The Negro lets him go: "I'm not going to give them an excuse to lynch me."

"Will you come and see me?" Miller asks Ewie. "Yes, on Saturday," she replies.

On the landing-stage, Ewie almost twists her ankles as she tries to walk in her oversize high-heels, and ends up by jumping gaily along as though she were playing hopscotch. Miller calls the Negro. "Your canoe is ready," he says.

So it is that Miller's love for a nymphette leads him to question his own racial prejudices, i.e. his whole conception of life, the world, and society. His previous moral code had seemed straightforward enough: two and two make four, one does not make love to little girls, one respects other people's property, Negroes are subhuman, and good is all on one side, with evil all on the other. But in fact nothing to do with mankind can be so simple or so natural. Our acts and our thoughts are above all distinguished by ambiguity, which does not of course mean that on the level of collective and individual praxis there is not the Right and the Left, the baddies and the non-baddies. I do not see any contradiction in these two statements because they do not work on the same level: a moral system based on ambiguity does not mean that unambiguous judgements may not be passed on men's actions, on the intentions that determine them and on the honesty that makes them authentic.

Buñuel narrates the story of *The Young One* with a subtle, wry touch and never allows himself to get carried away by the temptations of mere anti-racialist propaganda or of thematic variations on the *Lolita* theme. The direction of the film is full of little details that in the end are much more important than the story itself (a skinned rabbit hanging from a wall, soon destined for the stewpot, the fox in the hen-house, and the bottle of whiskey placed on Pee-Wee's grave, and so on). In spite of remaining throughout as realistic as an objective piece of reportage, the film does somehow manage to create a subtle atmosphere of poetry. The awkward, bouncy Ewie with her outsize shoes is the wonderfully variegated symbol that Buñuel offers up to our desire, so that we can confound the enemies of love and found an intelligible and radiant human order.

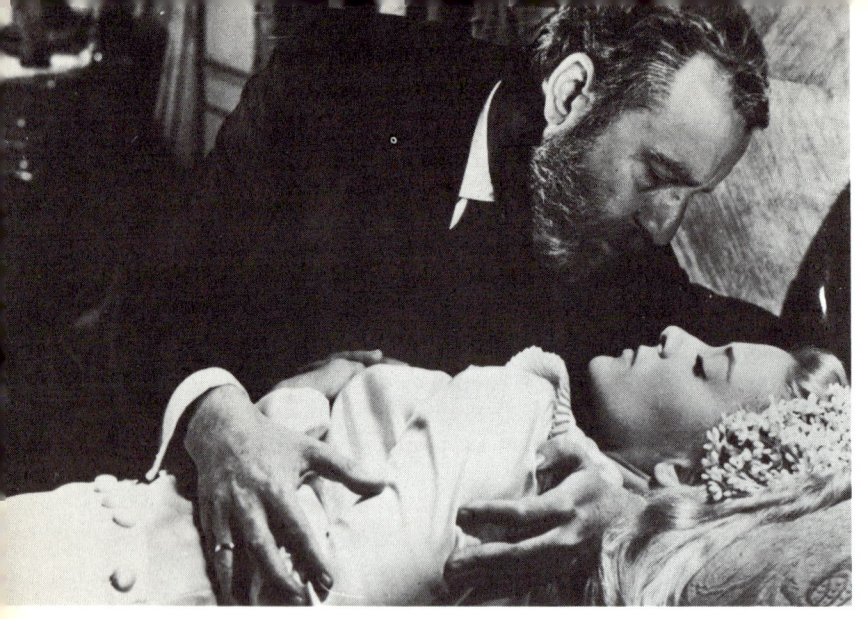

Fernando Rey with the drugged Silvia Pinal in VIRIDIANA

Viridiana

In November 1960, those who knew Buñuel were somewhat startled to learn that he had temporarily left Mexico for Spain, where he was planning to shoot a film. A number of perfidious rumours passed down the grapevine and ended up, garnished with suitably gloating innuendo, in the gossip columns of the French national newspapers: Buñuel was said to have given up his intransigently hostile attitude towards the Franco *régime*—an attitude which, up to then, had apparently only been shared by Pablo Casals and Picasso among internationally known celebrities (and how long, it was whispered, would *they* keep it up?). This opportunity was seized to carry out a surreptitious rehabilitation of the Spanish dictatorship under the cover of the "liberal tendencies" which Franco was supposedly encouraging.

The sort of people who broadcast these idiocies were either extremely naïve or (much more likely) hypocrites and liars. Only someone who had absolutely no inkling of Buñuel's warm-heartedness and honesty could possibly have believed that after spending twenty-five years in voluntary exile and directing the sort of films he had directed he would suddenly lose his fighting spirit.

If the man who made *Las Hurdes* decided to go back and make a film in his native country, one could be sure he had some pretty good reasons to do so. His true friends never doubted for a moment that he would produce a justification; and the justification was more convincing than they could have hoped. It was, quite simply, *Viridiana.*

The scenario of *Viridiana* was written by Buñuel himself in collaboration with Julio Alejandro (who had already worked with him on the script of *Nazarin,* and was later to do so on *Simon of the Desert* and *Tristana*). The film was originally supposed to be shot in Mexico for a young dynamic producer, Gustavo Alatriste, who sincerely admired Buñuel and was determined to give him complete freedom. Following an agreement he made with two Spanish production companies that had, on more than one occasion, courageously shown a determination to break away from the conformism of Spanish folklore and melodrama, Alatriste sounded Buñuel out on the possibility of a Spanish-Mexican co-production. For a long time Buñuel could not make up his mind; and when he did, it was probably partly because he wanted his personal prestige to help those who had made possible the shooting of Bardem and Berlanga's ¡Bienvenido Mister Marshall!, Bardem's Sonatas and A las Cinco de la Tarde, Saura's Los Golfos, and Ferreri's El Cochecito.

Buñuel naturally had to submit his script to the Spanish censorship board. With all the diligence of an obedient pupil, he agreed to all the changes in detail it suggested, and did not even object to changing the end of the film. This respectful attitude (superficially at least) of a man notorious for his explosiveness meant that the government supervisors of the film dropped their guard; they were delighted to be able to give the impression that (superficially at least!) theirs was a country of free speech.

In the spring of 1961, after the shooting was finished, Buñuel showed a cutting copy to the censors. Then he left for Paris to complete the editing and the mixing. Meanwhile he was invited to take part in the Cannes Film Festival on a personal basis. As the film was finally completed only a few days before the opening of the festival, the idea of sending a copy to Madrid for a censorship certificate was not even considered. Moreover, as no other Spanish film was being shown in competition, Viridiana was assumed to be Spain's official entry. And José Munoz-Fontan, the official representative of the Spanish film industry, failed to deny press reports to this effect. And so Viridiana, a Spanish film that was officially representing Spain, was shown on the last evening of the Festival, on May 17, 1961, the day before the Grand Prix was to be announced. The film proved such a bombshell that the jury, which had already drawn up a provisional list of prizewinners, was obliged to revise its ratings. Next day it awarded the Palme d'Or to *Viridiana* (*ex aequo* with Henri Colpi's *Une aussi longue absence;* Jerzy Kawalerowicz's *Mother Joan of the Angels* came in second place). Buñuel had stayed in Paris. So it was José Munoz-Fontan who proudly marched up on stage to receive the prize on his behalf. When he returned to Madrid, delighted that Spain had managed to notch up such an unexpected victory, he was hauled over the coals. The newspaper, *L'Osservatore Romano*, irritated by the warm reception given to Kawalerowicz's film, at once protested vigorously; *Viridiana* was the last straw. The mouthpiece of the Vatican described it as "sacrilegious and blasphematory." Like any self-respecting obedient Catholic, General Franco immediately took drastic measures. No mention was to be made of the film anywhere in the press, and Mr. Munoz-Fontan was briskly sent into the wilderness, to be replaced by one Mr. Sueros (whose Christian name was Jesus).

The banning of *Viridiana* in its own country created a situation where many people desperately tried to confuse the issue by reducing the whole affair to a question of distribution rights. Pressures of various kinds were brought to bear by the Spanish government on France and other countries. At one time it seemed almost as though this stateless film might never be commercially distributed. I remember a private showing that Buñuel organised, at my request, for fifteen or so people in a small viewing theatre on the Champs-Elysées; the people who were there—and they included Sartre, Simone de Beauvoir and Franju—all had the same feeling that they were taking part in some secret festival. It was almost a year later that *Viridiana* finally began its commercial career, thanks to the fact that it was officially recognised as being of a single nationality—Mexican. Its release created great enthusiasm as well as causing a good deal of sometimes violent animosity. The Belgian Union of Film Critics awarded it their Grand Prix, whereas in Italy, when an import licence was finally granted in 1963, the copies were seized and mutilated amid a chorus of hatred from religious circles.

It will be interesting, I think, from a documentary point of view, to quote one or two of the hostile reactions caused by the film. I have chosen, because they are typical in the worst sense of the word, two articles that appeared in Swiss papers. A few sentences will suffice to give some idea of the general tone. In the Geneva daily, *La Suisse:* "It is Buñuel's worst film—and it reeks of his senility. His fondness for obscenity and crude religious caricature, which may have seemed novel and quaint in *Un Chien Andalou* and other films of yore, seems extraordinarily antiquated when one encounters it thirty or forty years later in a contemporary film. How pathetic it all is, the caricature of *The Last Supper* which is just an excuse to show some repulsive beggars getting drunk, the sequence where an old man tries to seduce his niece, or the one in the cowshed, with its Freudian obscenity . . ." (16.1.62) And in *Le Peuple,* a socialist (!) daily printed in Lausanne: "After seeing his last film I feel that Buñuel, with all his complexes and obsessions with certain themes which he besmirches with a kind of inverted love, needs psychiatric treatment . . . All these anarchist and surrealist nobodies, whose elucubrations are as hazy as Jean Paulhan's are crystal clear, deserve nothing better than a straitjacket . . ." (24.2.62).

But I really ought to be getting down to brass tacks, i.e. to the masterpiece that is *Viridiana*.

In it, Buñuel remains faithful to everything he has ever said or stood for, synthesising in a quite startling manner the excessive violence and atrocities of *L'Age d'Or* and *Las Hurdes* with a new, more mature humanism. He is still a rebel who stands by his original principles, but he no longer needs to make his voice heard by having recourse to spectacular provocation. *Viridiana* encapsulates Buñuel's whole *Weltanschauung*. Good and evil are both fallacies that lead to dead ends. All acts are tinged to an equal

The "Last Supper" parody in VIRIDIANA

degree with ambiguity, and nothing will change so long as we still live with our present moral system, i.e. the denial of *amour fou* and the affirmation of mystifying abstract forces. In Buñuel's eyes, there is no point in saving either a dog or a soul so long as the psycho-social set-up encourages the enslavement of dogs and souls —which should not of course stop us saving a dog if ever we can. Such are the concentric parabolae of *Viridiana*, a film that relies less on intellectual argument than on hitting the spectator between the eyes. Once again Buñuel's detractors, the narrow-minded champions of a cinematic language that possesses a semantic specificity, are thoroughly wrong: more clearly than in his other films, the direction is much, much more than the mere visual translation of anecdotal or literary arguments that have been inventively arranged into a shooting script; it creates a magic combination where form and content fuse dialectically at white hot temperature. This is why the Spanish censors were so wrong in thinking they could tame Buñuel by supervising his scenario: he is an alchemist who is capable of producing sublime things from the most basic fiction.

Viridiana fits into the tradition of the picaresque novel. Certain scenes are strongly reminiscent of Goya, Bosch and Max Ernst (the last's creative techniques are used by Buñuel in the image of the beggars mimicking the attitudes of the characters in Leonardo Da Vinci's *The Last Supper,* with an ill-natured, treacherous and randy blind man sitting in Christ's seat).

The evolution of Viridiana, the film's central character, conditions the whole structure of this sacrilegious construction: shortly before taking her vows, she reluctantly leaves the convent in order to visit an old uncle whom she hardly knows, but who, according to the Mother Superior, has helped her considerably: "He has paid for your studies and for your keep; he has just sent the money you need to become a nun, and I fear that his health may not be too good." From this point on, her virtue is assailed by an inexorable series of misfortunes. After arriving at the farm, when she is preparing to go to bed, she undoes her blonde hair, which cascades on to her shoulders. Then as she slowly takes off her coarse cotton stockings she reveals the highly desirable flesh of her thighs. Like some plant that is capable of loosening the stones of a wall, the woman' in her seems likely to disrupt the overconfident behaviour of the pious nun, now that she is no longer protected from foreign eyes by the cloister. From this moment on, an irreversible process goes into motion: Viridiana is going to be born again to the world. Her uncle, Don Jaime, endlessly plays records of religious music. Up in the loft he still keeps the bridal dress of his wife, who died in his arms on their wedding night the very moment she was about to be possessed by him. He lovingly caresses the white satin dress and the orange-blossom crown, and puts on expensive shoes. He is particularly disturbed by Viridiana's presence because she resembles his dead wife.

With the help of Ramona, his faithful servant, he asks her to marry him. She is shocked, and refuses. But she does agree, however, to gratify just one apparently innocent desire of the old man: to appear before him dressed in bridal attire. With Ramona as accomplice, Don Jaime puts the girl to sleep by slipping a drug into her coffee, carries her to his bed, unbuttons her bodice, then finally gives up the idea of raping her. The whole scene is witnessed by Rita, Ramona's little girl, who has climbed a tree outside the window (we see her skipping at various times throughout the film). Next morning, Don Jaime attempts to extort his niece's consent by telling her that he possessed her while she was asleep. She runs away horrified. But just as she is getting on to the bus that is to take her back to the convent, she learns that a tragedy has just occurred: Don Jaime has hanged himself with Rita's skipping-rope. Viridiana returns to the farm. She feels somehow responsible for the old man's suicide and considers herself to be lost to the Church. But her religious belief remains unshaken. She tries to put it into practice by becoming a kind of solitary apostle, rather in the same way as Nazarin, but with a clearer desire to prove effective: she decides to relieve the suffering of her neighbour.

But far from straightening out matters, her charity, though sincere, results in a series of catastrophes. A group of beggars who have become the young evangelist's *protégés* refuse to play ball: they are unwilling to accept gaily the redeeming suffering and all its rules and regulations which she tries to impose on them. Quite rightly, they have no respect at all for the pity she bestows on them when she is not murmuring a prayer or singing the praises of hard work. This gang of Hurdanos take advantage of her absence to give free rein to their instincts and ransack the house. They unfold tablecloths, lay the table, eat off the most expensive crockery, and fornicate in a corner. One of them dresses up in the underclothes and veil of the bride, and dances grotesquely to the strains of religious music.

Because she wanted to be an angel, in other words because she

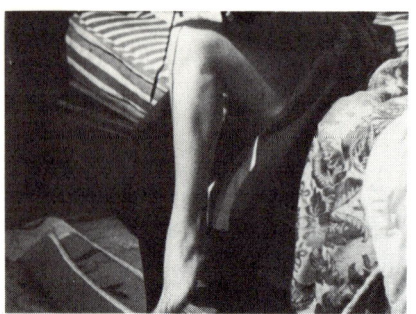 

Foot (or thigh) fetichism in VIRIDIANA

had refused to be a woman, Viridiana again risks rape: when she returns home, her drunken *protégés* do their very best to have it off with her. In the end, Viridiana comes full circle—from religious resignation to social resignation. To a background of jazz, we see her accept the *ménage à trois* imposed on her by Don Jaime's son, Jorge, a liberated, realistic and slightly cynical architect who came back to the farm after his father's death and promptly took Ramona as a mistress.

This black comedy, played out to the accompaniment of Handel's *Messiah*, has all the density of a poem. All the obsessions that colour Buñuel's universe have been meticulously worked into the film. Take foot fetichism, for example: most of the characters are at some time or other shown from the ankle down. One should also note Don Jaime's fixation on his dead wife's shoes, and also his way of staring at Rita's dancing little feet as she skips.

With each new image—the keyholes, the jumble of objects in

the loft where the cat leaps on the mouse, the skein of wool that is thrown on to the fire, the handful of ashes placed on the bed, the crucifix-cum-flick-knife, the stove burning the crown of thorns, the skipping-rope (with which, as I have said, Don Jaime hangs himself, and which is later used as a belt by one of the beggars), and the bridal veil that is trampled on—Buñuel takes us further into a thoroughly recognisable mental universe, where nature and artifice, the profane and the sacred, spells and exorcisms all fuse in a tremendous farrago of incongruous objects and unusual, multi-purpose instruments which are either symbolic, not symbolic, or potentially symbolic. In other words, it is a sick human world which is all the more frightening because traditional moral categories are disappearing, a world that could be compared, if you like, to the leper in the film who "sticks his arm into the holy water so as to pass on his disease to women," who drags a tin can with him wherever he goes to stop healthy people coming near him, and who cannot be cured by prayers. As is shown in the swinging Angelus sequence, each verse of soothing celestial praise is irreparably shattered as it is contrasted with the constructive, tiring actions of our earthly existence. This is constantly being brought home to Viridiana. Her goodness comes up against realities of which she was unaware when she naïvely took refuge in the moral ivory tower of Christian faith. When she asks for some milk, she is told she can draw it herself from the cow. As her hand takes hold of the udder, she discovers both the animal and a particular shape that she again encounters when she picks up the phallic handle of the skipping rope and will also feel, presumably, when she goes to bed with Jorge after the end of the film. She will not then of course be a saved woman. But at least she will have achieved the basic carnal truth on which, because of guilt and fear of sin, she had so resolutely turned her back.

The fire and brimstone of *Viridiana* seem to have flowed in an effortless surge from Buñuel's subconscious. In an interview with

Yvonne Baby,[26] he explained the creative process of making the film:

"I didn't deliberately set out to be blasphemous, but then Pope John XXIII is a better judge of such things than I am. It is only by chance that I happen to show some ungodly images; if I had godly ideas maybe I might express them. When you're sixty-one, you're not interested in behaving childishly, and as I have no preconceived position I refuse to get caught up in the scandal surrounding my film. In *Viridiana* I have remained true to the ideas I have always expressed ever since *L'Age d'Or*, and although thirty years separate them they are the two films where I have had the greatest creative freedom. Not all my films are equally successful, and I have made some pretty commonplace ones in order to earn a living. But I have always refused to make compromises and have always stuck up for the ideas in which I believe. I went back to Spain because it is my country and because I was able to work in complete freedom there.

"Viridiana was a little-known saint who lived at the time of St. Francis of Assisi. I was struck by her name a long time ago. When I was in Mexico, the story came to me. As with all my films, it began with an image, then the rest of the film flowed quite naturally from there."

"What was the image in this case?"

"A young woman 'drugged' by an old man: she is then at the mercy of somebody who in normal circumstances would never have been able to keep her in his arms. It occurred to me that the woman should be pure, so I made her a novice. The idea of the beggars came afterwards: it struck me as natural that they should be welcomed by a former nun into her house. Then I decided I would like to see these beggars having a feast in the dining-room at a huge table covered with an embroidered tablecloth and candlesticks. I suddenly realised that they were seated as if in a painting, and I consciously alluded to Leonardo Da

Vinci's *Last Supper*. Then I accompanied the orgy and the dance of the beggars with the Hallelujah chorus from Handel's *Messiah*, which I thought would create a much more striking effect than rock-and-roll music. I liked the effect. Similarly I decided to use Mozart's *Requiem* as the background to the love scene between the old man and the girl, and to contrast the gentle chanting of the Angelus with shots of workers sweating away."

"What images have you been particularly criticised for?"

"The blazing crown of thorns, though burning is not desecration as far as I know. People have attacked me for showing a knife in the shape of a crucifix. But such knives can be found all over Spain, and I've seen lots of them in Albacete. My sister, who is very religious, once met a nun who used this sort of knife to peel apples with. So it wasn't I who invented the "flick-knife Christ." The photography alone brings out the irony and the surrealist quality of an object that is mass-produced in all innocence."

The Exterminating Angel

Viridiana, with its direct thematic link with *L'Age d'Or*, was, one would have thought, Buñuel's masterpiece to end all masterpieces. It was hard to imagine how a more devastating attack on disciplinary conventions, constraining mystiques, and the blatant colonisation of hearts, minds, and sexual organs, could possibly be made in view of the film industry's organisation and its economico-intellectual kowtowing to a state-controlled moral code. But genius has a way of always managing to go one further than one would have thought possible. Buñuel did precisely this, and with quite extraordinary straight-forwardness, thanks again to Gustavo Alatriste, the producer of *Viridiana*.

Buñuel and his friend, Luis Alcoriza, had written a scenario loosely based on *Los Naufragos*, a very slight short story by the

Catholic Spanish writer, and friend of Georges Bernanos, José Bergamín. Buñuel called his film version *The Castaways of Providence Street*, and planned to shoot it in 1957, before making *Nazarin*. But circumstances prevented him from doing so. After a wait of a few years, he went back to the script, and made it into *The Exterminating Angel*. When it was shown at the Cannes Film Festival of 1962, the jury was so flummoxed by its poetry that they awarded the Grand Prix to a Brazilian film, Anselmo Duarte's *The Given Word*, which superficially was quite Buñuelesque but utterly different ideologically. The International Federation of Film Critics (FIPRESCI) was more intelligent and managed to make the official attribution of prizes look a little less asinine by awarding its own prize to *The Exterminating Angel*. A month later, the film won another award at the Rassegna del Cinema Latino-Americano in Sestri-Levante, which resulted in its being included in the programme of the "Festival of Festivals" in Acapulco. When I re-saw the film there, I was flabbergasted by the indifference shown by the public and by a number of Mexican film critics, particularly in view of its relevance to themselves.

It should be said from the start that those who like the empty beauty and flashy "modernity" of fashionable not-so-New Wave directors will probably find the film disconcerting and incomprehensible.

Basically, the plot could not be more banal. But its expressive form is such that realism and fiction combine to produce pure fantasy without the film's ever being anything but everyday. Its development has an inexorable logic about it that generates an extraordinary mixture of fear and humour. The event in the film that acts as a catalyst ends up by completely destroying the social structure: in the devastated landscape that results from it, not a single trace of a past order or of a previous illusion remains. The self-destructive process of the consumer society reaches its highest pitch of degradation.

Guests at dawn in THE EXTERMINATING ANGEL

The signs of our civilisation—a convenient mirage that used to conceal the disorder of human life—vanish, and at last we come into contact with reality. But it is too late: all is rotten. Beneath the bandages of religious consolation and reassuring ethical laws, the wound has begun to fester, and the whole organism is incurably infected. Everywhere exchange values have been replaced by utility values. The diabolical syndrome of physical and psychological destitution as displayed by the Hurdanos no longer spares the well-fed bourgeois, who fall victim to an identical curse of their own making, and experience the same moral decay. The difference is that the imbeciles are no longer skulking among barren rocks, as in *Las Hurdes,* but crawling along at 5 m.p.h. in traffic jams at the wheels of cars designed to be driven at 100 m.p.h.

The Exterminating Angel is not a film that can be "explained." Juan-Luis Buñuel has said: "My father said to me: 'If you're asked why there are so many repetitions at the beginning of the film, you should say it is because the film was too short to start with. In fact, there are at least twenty repetitions in the film, which is only normal—people are repetitious in real life too. One shouldn't go on a wild goose chase for explicit symbols. It is a very personal film, and things that may be taken as symbols are more often than not merely memories. For instance, what the woman sees from the lavatory is quite simply the town of Cuenca, where the lavatories are on a cliff and where a valley, a river and some birds can in fact be seen through the hole. Why don't they want to leave the room in the film? Now there's a difficult question. We never know whether they can't or whether they don't want to, do we?' "[27]

So one has, of course, to beware of the sort of oversimplified interpretation which fatuously supposes that the film is a mechanically coded transposition of a pre-existing clear-cut message and that one needs only to know the cipher in order to understand.

The language of the man who made *L'Age d'Or* and *The Exterminating Angel* follows none of the rules of any "cinematurgy" of angles, cuts, and syntactical complexes that restrict the scope for intellectual montage. His basic ingredients, here even more than ever, are ordinary, directly informative vocabulary and intuitively functional grammar of the kind that might be used by a child at kindergarten. But like the child, "he revels in experimenting with this heritage as though it were all a game. He strings words together without caring about their meaning, just for the pleasure of rhythm and rhyme."[28]

Freud's analysis in *Jokes and Their Relation to the Unconscious* is of considerable use when one tries to understand Buñuel's creative processes and his way of escaping the desert of pure reason by surreptitiously opening the flood-gates of the irrational. He knows Freud's theories well, and has great fun getting involved in his little game. Controlled skids in the plot are the prelude to unexpected, uncontrolled and uncontrollable behaviour. Snatches of dialogue, juxtaposed according to reflexes conditioned by etiquette manuals and by general reasonableness, take on the scathing sharpness of surrealist proverbs—or of the surrealist poems that were written in the least "literary" manner, i.e. those of Benjamin Péret. There is no longer any distinction between a spectacle and its vision, or between the surveyor's measurements and a mental picture. Elsewhere, whenever Buñuel makes preposterous pictorial allusions (the guffawing Christ during Andara's delirium in *Nazarin*, Da Vinci's *Last Supper* in *Viridiana*, and Millet's *L'Angélus* in *Belle de jour*), his aim is always the same: to destroy our mental sclerosis through anxiety, surprise or humour, and to rejuvenate our way of seeing and thinking in much the same way as Marcel Duchamp did when he raised a bottle-rack to the status of a work of art.

All this brings me back to *The Exterminating Angel*, which certainly takes the spectator off the beaten track. Nobile and his wife, rich Mexican aristocrats, arrive back at their luxurious home with some friends to have supper after the opera. Hardly have they set foot in the hall before the invisible angel of the bizarre slips amongst them. The servants leave the house, or no longer answer the bell when they are called. Then, slowly, the fine party manners and the chitchat ebb and flow between the strange and the routine. "Excuse me if I change the order of the menu. We are going to start with a Maltese dish. According to the traditions of the island, it is served as a hors-d'oeuvre because it apparently whets the appetite. Liver! Honey! Almonds! And lashings of spices in the sauce!" the hostess says abruptly, chipping in on a discussion about one's country: "One's country is a group of rivers that flow into the sea. The sea that is death. There you are . . . to die for one's country." The faithful butler stumbles as he carries in the first dish and is sent sprawling to the ground. "Oh Lucia, how delightful! Frightfully unexpected . . . Lucia has a knack for this sort of surprise," exclaim the guests. During the meal, incongruous remarks are exchanged banteringly: "Why did she kiss you so passionately? Poor Leonora. And how is her cancer? Is there any hope?" "None. I would say that in barely three months she will have gone completely bald" (in other words, dead). "She has a good skull," concludes one of the guests.

The bearded old conductor (who looks as though he had escaped from *L'Age d'Or*) does not feel too well and lies down. The

"*The psychosis worsens.*" THE EXTERMINATING ANGEL

end of the evening looks very promising. A beautiful young woman throws an ashtray at the window. "A Jew was walking by," comes the dead-pan explanation. Blanca plays a sonata by Paradisi on the piano. Everybody goes into raptures. A woman opens her handbag and takes out a handkerchief and two chicken's feet. The atmosphere gets sticky, and the party is overtaken by a kind of listlessness. Some make movements to leave. But no one wants or is able to leave the room. Everybody settles down to a kind of improvised camp life in armchairs, and on the carpets and divans. They make themselves utterly at ease. Dinner jackets are taken off. The lights are turned out. Hands grope for each other. Lovers embrace.

At dawn, everybody tries to put a good normal face on things again. But both their faces and their clothes are crumpled. Quite inexplicably, it is impossible for anybody to cross the threshold in order to fetch some tea-spoons from the pantry. "Why didn't you go out? Just to be like other people!" The Angel of the bizarre has now definitely given way to the Exterminating Angel. "We've been here for a good twenty-four hours, and no one has come. We have been forgotten." "The attitude of people outside worries me more than our own predicament. What's the matter with them? They ought to have tried to do something about . . ." "Unless of course everyone else in the town is dead and we are the last survivors . . ." A thirsty man is given water to drink from a vase of flowers. "Above all let's not lose our heads, gentlemen. Nothing is worse than panic . . . if we coolly analyse what is happening to us, we'll be able to come to terms with our aboulia." But there is no real reaction, only one or two general remarks, a few platitudes, and the occasional flare-up of hurt pride. Time passes. Social conventions slowly disintegrate. A man dies, and his body is put in a cupboard which serves as a refuge for the two lovers, who end up by committing suicide together. The psychosis worsens. There is nothing left to drink. The situation becomes nightmarish. The severed hand from *Un Chien Andalou* is seen lying on the floor and creates panic. Good manners begin to give way to the instinct of self-preservation. A curious crowd gathers in front of the house. Firemen attempt a rescue operation, but are unable to get into the house. All channels of communication are cut. Inside, those who still have any strength play the role of pioneers, taking up the parquet floor and hacking away at concrete in the hope of finding the mains. When water gushes out, there is rejoicing, and a fleeting return to good behaviour: "The women first!" People eat paper. "Paper does not taste at all unpleasant, señorita. My friends and I used to eat it when we were children. Maybe it was because we got bored at school. I was educated by the Jesuits. A decent lot, they were! We got bored, like most children I suppose. Paper is good . . . Apparently it's made of the leaves and tender bark of trees. It can't do any harm. Would you like to taste a bit?" Little by little, an atmosphere of mutual contempt can be sensed; people's consciences get caught up in the toils of worry and fear; and in the end, within a short space of time, the whole group has sunk to the level of the Hurdanos. They are not so much Robinson Crusoes as the collective version of Francisco in *El*. They are incapable of knowing themselves, and therefore of recognising each other; they are incapable of stripping away their own clinging bourgeois *façade* and revealing the naked man beneath; they are seized by panic when they realise that the individual has been devoured by the canker of Christian civilisation; and in their eyes the last possibility of hypothetical salvation lies in beseeching God to bring about a miracle. In the blindness of their hearts and minds they fail to see that the real miracle lies within them. Or maybe they pretend not to see this because they know that if they accept this obvious fact they will also have to accept the right to freedom of all those people who do not belong to their class, of all those Man Fridays after the return to England. They prefer to die rather than give up their privileges. But first they still hope that divine grace will swoop down on them, and to encourage it to do so they make solemn pledges: "If we manage to get out of this fix, if I recover, I want to go to Lourdes with you. You promise to come with me, don't you? We will go and throw ourselves at the feet of the Virgin Mary—she's the only person who can get us out of here. When we get to Lourdes, I want you to buy me a washable rubber Virgin. You *will* buy me one, won't you?" They even consider having recourse to cabalistic rituals and shedding the innocent blood which alone can obtain the remission of one's sins. In their prayers, they work themselves up into a visionary state: "The Pope! Yes, it's him. How impressive and majestic he is! He looks like a warrior." A few moments later, somebody dares to bring up the classical theory of the scapegoat that lies at the base of hysterical anti-Communism, anti-semitism, and all other kinds of witch-hunting: "Raul has told me that if Nobile dies all this will end. Once the spider dies, the web falls to pieces. If he had any self-respect he would realise what his duty was." "You want to do away with him? But you must have gone mad! The idea is quite insane and irrational!" "We are not interested in what is rational, we want to get out of here." At this point in their panic-stricken lunacy, the doctor intervenes:

The Doctor:	"Listen to me, you madmen!
Ana:	"Kill the doctor at the same time. He must have his reasons for trying to stop us . . .
The Doctor:	"Think of the terrible consequences of what you intend to do! This dastardly murder will not be the last. It presupposes the disintegration of our human dignity and our transformation into wild animals."

This clear warning is their one chance. Will they have the sense to seize it? Back in their original positions, they behave and converse just as they had before the bewitchment. Blanca again plays the Paradisi sonata; and they go out.

But they do not seize their chance; they do not learn the lesson of their painful yet potentially instructive sojourn on the raft of *The Medusa*. After their experiences they ought to have felt "proud of themselves as men." But the thing they feel the greatest urge to do is in fact to reject the new life that is open to them—a life where a whole wonderful new future remains to be built and where, because God no longer has any meaning, all is possible. They refuse to be stripped of their insincerity, their sense of guilt and their poisonous metaphysical obligations; instead, they go and fall on their knees in church, where the exterminating Angel can again spread its wings. Yet again, there is a bewitching attraction in becoming cloistered. As the bells ring, a flock of sheep trots into the church in preparation for the holocaust. Outside, there are riots; policemen shoot. The rebels ask us to come with them to the barricades in order to prepare tomorrow's liberation. It is up to us to answer in the affirmative or else to decide to take refuge with the gullible, plague-ridden wretches in the cathedral, which sports a yellow flag, the traditional signal to healthy ships that one has sick people on board.

There are countless other beautiful details to be found in this grey dream of a film, so superbly photographed by Figueroa; and the spectator should be allowed to appreciate them for himself. All that need be said is that the occasionally glimpsed bear in no way stands for the Soviet Union. As Buñuel said to J. F. Aranda in this connection: "People always want an explanation for everything. It's the logical result of centuries of bourgeois education. And when they can't explain something, they end up by turning to God. But what good does that do them? They then have to explain God. As for myself, I simply cannot change the way I am. I have not been blessed with the faith. I'm afraid that a life that includes ambiguities and contradictions interests me. Mystery is beautiful. I can't see anything wrong in dying and disappearing from the face of the earth. The idea that I might be eternal fills me with horror. For example, if my best friend, who died a long time ago, appeared before me and touched my ear with his fingers and immediately set fire to it, even then I wouldn't believe that he had just come from Hell. Nor would I have any greater belief in God, or in the Immaculate Conception of the Virgin; nor would I think that the Virgin could help me pass my exams. I would simply say to myself: 'Luis, look, this is just another mystery that you can't understand.' "[29]

After the Angel

Buñuel returned to Madrid in November 1962 with the intention of shooting a film there. The Spanish authorities assured him that he would be able to work without any kind of hindrance whatever. In so many words, they agreed that as *Viridiana* and the scandal it had caused were forgotten bygones should be bygones. What is more, censorship had apparently become more "democratic"! So Buñuel planned to make a film consisting of four episodes, which would be called *Four Mysteries*. (He had dropped the idea of adapting Valle Inclan's *Divinas Palabras*, as well as Tirano Banderas and Dostoevsky's *The Eternal Husband*.) According to what Buñuel told J. F. Aranda, these four mysteries would have been the following:

Aura, after a short story by the Mexican writer Carlos Fuentes.

The Maenads, after the Argentinian writer, Julio Cortazar.

Gradiva, after Wilhelm Jensen's short novel, to which Freud devoted a lengthy psycho-analytical commentary. Published in 1903, the story concerns a young German scientist, called Hanold, who is deeply disturbed by the bodily harmony, and above all by the gracefully positioned feet, of a young woman featured on a basrelief that he finds in a collection of antiques in Rome. He has a plaster cast made and hangs it on the wall of his bedroom. He is fascinated by the woman: he dreams about her, thinks he sees her in the street, and goes to Pompeii because it was there that he saw her in one of his nightmares. Among the ruins there, he meets, alternately, a very real young woman and the phantasma that obsesses him. In his delirium he confuses the two; in the end he manages to free himself by means of a childhood memory. He finally takes responsibility for the love he has for this young woman, who is called Zoé, and is thereby able to project on her all the desire that Gravida, the creature on the bas-relief, had fired in him. As the couple leave Pompeii, the young scientist is finally and completely cured when he sees Zoé, who is walking in front of him, in an attitude that coincides just for a second with that of Gravida. Just as one can remember something one has forgotten by going back to the moment of one's forgetting, and just as the beleaguered party-goers in *The Exterminating Angel* escape their imaginary prison by repeating the movements and attitudes that immediately led up to their predicament, the scientist again takes a grip on himself and his responsibilities: as he walks down the sunny, paved streets of the ghost city, he reminds one of Arcibaldo de la Cruz after he has thrown his musical box into the river.

The last of the Four Mysteries was, according to Buñuel, "to be bitingly humorous and the most subjective of them all—a very personal, subject, something to do with the kidnapping of a little girl."

He hoped to start shooting in March 1963. Meanwhile, he had decided to replace one of the episodes by another one, and even to add a further episode he had written with Juan Larrea: *The Illegible Son of Flute*. But the project as a whole had to be postponed. A producer suggested to Buñuel that he adapt another novel by Galdós, the author of *Nazarin*, and his choice fell on *Tristana*. Everything seemed ready for the film to get under way during the summer of 1963. But at the last moment the Franco government withheld its permission to shoot. So Buñuel's year in Spain in 1963 was completely barren, unless one counts the small role he agreed to play in Carlos Saura's film, *Llanto por un Bandido*. He plays an executioner who kills a condemned man with the mediaeval method for which the Caudillo still evinces a distinct partiality: garrotting. It was no coincidence that Buñuel agreed to play this part: he wanted in this way to draw attention to this sort of butchery at a time when, just after the execution of Julian Grimau, the western press was beginning, if only gingerly, to talk about the disgraceful behaviour of the Spanish Fascist dictatorship.

In spite of his international prestige, Buñuel continued to run into difficulties with his projects in Spain. He was forced to abandon a number of films, at various stages of preparation. These included *Thérèse Etienne*, after John Knittel, *La Femme et le pantin*, after Pierre Louys, *Le Hussard sur le toit*, after Jean Giono, and one of his favourite projects, M. K. Lewis's *The Monk*.

Buñuel did some more character acting, appearing in 1964 in a film by the young Mexican critic and director, Alberto Isaac, called *En Este Pueblo No Hay Ladrones* (*There Are No Thieves in This Village*). The plot is intentionally stark and free of dramatic complications, so as to enable the director to give a varied description of daily life in a poor village. Isaac is obviously inspired not only by *Los Olvidados* but also by Fellini's *I vitelloni*. In one sequence, the priest of the parish, played by Luis Buñuel, treats his congregation to a fiery, threatening sermon in the best tradition of hot-gospelling. And then the narrative continues in its unruffled way.

The Diary of a Chambermaid

As he found it impossible to shoot either *The Four Mysteries* or *Tristana* in Spain, Buñuel fell back on an old idea that he thought he had given up for good: an adaptation of Octave Mirbeau's *Le Journal d'une femme de chambre* (*The Diary of a Chambermaid*).

He prepared the shooting script in collaboration with Jean-Claude Carrière in Madrid during the months of July and August 1963, and shot the film in and around Paris during the winter of 1963/64.

Buñuel's return to French studios and Jeanne Moreau's admiring remarks about her director excited some expectancy in the press: several sensational stories in the papers trumpeted the news that Buñuel's film was going to be a scandalous masterpiece. But when it came out in March 1964, *The Diary of a Chambermaid* got a lukewarm reception. Most critics rather turned up their noses at it, while at the same time expressing, in condescending tones, their great admiration for the director's glorious past and for the performances of the two main actors. There was talk of sham violence, punch-pulling, and facile attacks on Aunt Sallies—as though in comparison the French cinema spent its time turning out aggressive pamphlets with a social conscience (in fact everyone knows—although Parisian critics, the most intellectually snobbish and chauvinistic in the world, are extremely loth to admit it—that the French cinema as a whole is notable for its lack of audacity when it comes to political or social subjects). As usual, then, the critics hummed and hawed, casually discussing the film's form while carefully avoiding any mention of its content: "The novel is execrable, and the film is not good. How is it (. . .) that one feels not only disappointed but embarrassed?" wrote Claude Mauriac, in *Le Figaro Littéraire* (12.3.64), without ever going on to answer this most pertinent question. Jean-Louis Bory, in *Arts* (11.3.64), revelled in his punchline: "Mirbeau is not there and Buñuel is absent," whereas *Combat* (5.3.64), waffled on about "old-fashioned naturalism" and did its best to disguise its sense of shock with the pirouette: "No, Luis Buñuel, you can do better than this."

In fact, the film is extremely well-balanced, intentionally stark, and carries a nasty direct punch. It would be an enormous mistake to consider the subject out-of-date. It has simply undergone a necessary process of enlargement that in many ways comes close

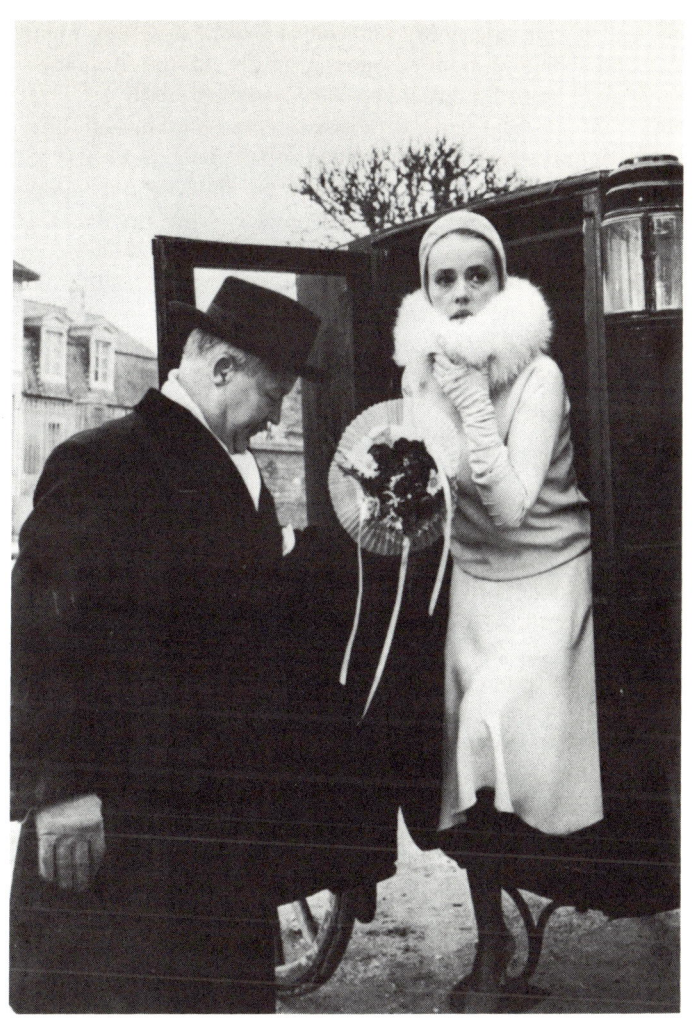

Célestine arrives at The Priory in DIARY OF A CHAMBERMAID

to Brecht's alienation effect. My allusion to Brecht is, I feel, highly relevant. Louis Seguin pointed most usefully to the similarities between Buñuel and Brecht when he remarked, with reference to *Nazarin:* "Because he want to alleviate men's ills through charity, he only aggravates the situations in which he intervenes, just as Mother Courage causes the death of her children by being a profiteer in an abstract war. The comparison with Brecht is no coincidence. *Nazarin* too is a work concerned with non-intervention, and its purpose is to denounce its most nefarious manifestation —the Christian attitude. The only attitude a priest has, or ever can have in the best of circumstances, is the submissive one described by the worker in *Señora Carrar's Rifles:* 'The attitude people have when they claim they do not accept something is terribly similar to the attitude they have when they capitulate.' "[30] The theatre critic, Bernard Dort, has also made an interesting comparison between Brecht's *St. Joan of the Stockyards* and *Viridiana*. He said, in conclusion: "With Brecht, the denunciation of individualism and spirituality forms part of an overall social struggle; with Buñuel, it is the result of deep historical pessimism. What makes them so different is the gulf between the revolutionary Germany of the Thirties and Spain of the Sixties. But although Brecht and Buñuel are very different, they tread similar paths: the message of both of them is that realism can only stem from a fundamental challenging of the fictional hero's romanticism."[31]

These remarks apply very well to *Viridiana*, but less so to *The Diary of a Chambermaid* (they were written one year before the film came out). By bringing forward Mirbeau's story by twenty-five years, Buñuel is able to tackle a historically defined society where Fascism is no longer simply a state of mind plus a few isolated violent actions, but something that makes itself felt very strongly, and numerically, in the streets. In this very way, his film takes on a militant anti-Establishment character which Arthur Adamov once described to me in an interview as quite exemplary: he said that Buñuel's film corresponded exactly to the sort of thing he himself was trying to say in the theatre. But one should not allow the parallels between the work of Brecht and Buñuel to mislead one into making the sort of generalisations that are better left to eager thesis writers and glib structuralist cosmetologists. For although the work of both of them centres on the same struggle against oppression, it is informed by two very different ways of thinking which cannot be perfunctorily boiled down to a single practical approach. Buñuel, if you like, is a seer on the march, while Brecht is a far-sighted marcher.

Jean Renoir adapted Mirbeau's novel in 1946 during his stay in Hollywood; he found it somewhat difficult to re-create in the studio the atmosphere and landscape of the end of the last century and the mores of the Third Republic and of a family of landed proprietors. Buñuel, by skipping a few years, is able to depict a time when the Jeunesses Catholiques, the Ligue des Patriotes and the antisemitic Ligue Antijuive made a commando raid on the Studio 28 cinema, baying: "We'll see if there are any Christians left in France," or "Death to the Jews!" *Le Figaro* wrote: "Come on, Monsieur Chiappe [the then Préfet de Police], put our house in order. You *can* do it and you *must* do it." Chiappe then published the official ban on *L'Age d'Or*.

Although Buñuel's adaptation is very free, and only draws on one episode from Mirbeau's book, he gets much closer to the spirit of the writer than does Renoir. True, there is definitely a certain charm about Renoir's smooth, satiny style, and about the way he counterpoints the deceptive happiness of the wealthy with lugubrious and cynical undertones and with a general odour of decay. Madame closes the shutters so as not to hear noises of the outside world or the blaring bands of July 14—an anniversary which, in her eyes, celebrates the date when France began to decline. But Célestine, although prepared to do anything in order to gain social advancement (when she arrives at The Priory, she has written in

 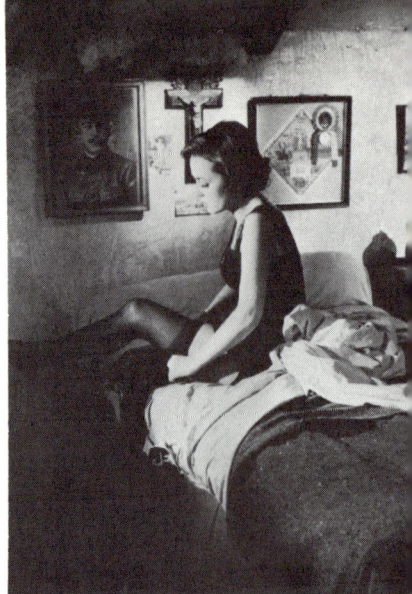

Jeanne Moreau with Georges Géret on the set of DIARY OF A CHAMBER-MAID (left), and in reflective mood in the film itself

her notebook: "From now on, no more love for Célestine," which indicates that all her acts will henceforth be coolly carried out solely with their usefulness in mind), ends up by requiting the love of the son of the family, a quixotic character who has revolted against his background. As a result, although the film is in some ways reminiscent of *La Règle du jeu*, it ends with a sentimental device that rather takes the punch out of what has preceded.

Mirbeau's book can be seen almost as a prelude to the affair of the Papin sisters, a preface to Jean Genet's *The Maids* and to *Les Abysses*, the film directed by Nico Papatakis from Jean Vauthier's script, or even as a vast portrait gallery of characters taken from Maupassant's short story, *Rosalie* (which Walerian Borowczyk has made into a film). But the relationship between master and slave, in the book, remains a tangled confusion within a completely rotten microcosm which still retains some semblance of unitarian hierarchy. The main principles—Work, Family and Country, and their corollaries, Capital, Church and Army—still carry enough weight to clamp down the lid of the pressure-cooker. Quite logically, the safety valve is the same both for the bosses and for the servants: they do not attribute their feeling of uneasiness to the moral, social and psychological structures that govern the order in which they believe. On the contrary, they attribute it, in order to escape responsibility for their own corruption, to imaginary forces which they feel are corrupting them. The situation is the same as the one described in *The Exterminating Angel*, but is in the end vectorially reversed. The clan of The Priory, like the people who are invited by the Nobiles of Providence Street, need scapegoats. For both of them, the Nazi mystique plus a dash of Christianity is what leavens their power urges.

Célestine is smart in both senses of the word. At the beginning of Buñuel's film, she takes the train to take up her new situation as chambermaid with the Rabour-Monteils. A man-servant is waiting for her on the platform of the station where she gets off the train, and drives her in a cabriolet to The Priory. "What's your name?" she asks. "Joseph," he answers. "That's the last straw," Célestine decides.

There are plenty of surprises in store for her at the château. Madame Monteil is a shrivelled woman in every way, stingy as well as being a stickler for tidiness. She complains to the priest that her husband is much too demanding: "Twice a week, Father!" "But that's much, much too often!" exclaims the messenger of God. And he adds: "I mean to say, the thing is that *you* shouldn't get any pleasure out of it." "Oh, Father, you needn't worry, there's no likelihood of that!"

Her husband is a frustrated man who spends his time either hunting or putting buns in the ovens of the successive maids who come to work at the house. He openly states that his wife has ruined his life; and each time he gets the urge to have it off with a cook or a servant-girl, he stomps round in circles muttering, among other things, "*I am all for l'amour fou!*"—a remark which, coming from a randy nitwit like him, is hilariously ironic. And as for grandfather Rabour (Madame Monteil's father), he is an old fuddy-duddy who divides his time between the garden, where we see him firing a gun at the butterflies who pillage his flowers, and his bedroom, where he thumbs through bulky old albums and tends to his invaluable collection of women's boots. Practically the only pleasure left to this fetichist is to see a dainty pair of feet putting on his treasured boots; the moment they get dirty (which gives him further pleasure), he sets about cleaning them and giving them a good shine (which gives him the greatest kick of all).

Down in the pantry, where we see two women chasing a mouse with their brooms, life is not much more savoury. Here, Joseph is king of the castle. He is as hard as nails and seems not to have a single weakness. He is a militant member of a right-wing organisation and makes no secret of his opinions, particularly when he is visited by a sacristan who shares his beliefs. To his mind, the country will go to the dogs unless some steps are taken to remedy the situation, such as kicking out all foreigners and Jews. In this way the nation will be rid of those bastards in cloth caps, who are said to have recently held protest meetings with a view to pressing wage claims. "The ministers, the successive governments, and the judges," says the sacristan, "have all sold their souls, the whole bloody lot of them! And they've sold them to the Jews! That's why everything's in such a mess. One doesn't have to look very far: scratch a Bolshie and you'll find a Jew. And now people are laying into religion again." When he hears the sacristan say this, Joseph reacts: "Don't expect me to stand up and defend the clergy, but I'm all for religion! One simply can't get by without religion . . ."

But after a little friendly persuasion from the sacristan, he changes his mind and resigns himself to accepting the clergy as the lesser of two evils. The sacristan cuts a lot of ice with his peremptory statement: "The clergy will help us to get rid of the Jews."

Quite apart from his strict conception of what the country and its discipline should be, this true blue cherishes the secret hope of one day being able to open a bistro in Cherbourg, a good place for business because it is a garrison town. His establishment will be called "A l'Armée Française," and the dishy Célestine will draw the customers. But Joseph also has a decidedly sadistic bent: when he kills geese he likes to make them suffer, and sometimes he stares at a little girl called Claire in a most peculiar way. One day he says to her: "Look at me hard and straight in the eyes. Like this . . . What can you see?" "I can see myself," she answers. "That proves that I'm fond of you, you understand. That proves that I think about you . . ." And while he is walking through the woods he meets the little girl, who is collecting snails, and loses control. The child is later found dead, covered with blood and sexually assaulted, with snails crawling up her rigid little legs.

When the crime is discovered, no one except Célestine suspects the man-servant. She goes to his bedroom and offers herself to him in the hope that once having slept with her he will confide in her. He refuses to touch her, adding: "Of course I would if it were just for a bit of fun!" But he feels seriously about her and stands by his right-wing principles. He has the same combination of anticlericalism and sexual frivolousness as Don Lope in *Tristana* —an attitude which, on the contrary, "when it's serious" requires that there should be no love-making before a priest has blessed the union. Joseph talks to Célestine about their marriage and their café in Cherbourg: "You're just the right sort of orderly woman I need. You're nice too, and you stick up for yourself. No doubt about it, you'll have all those soldiers under your thumb." "So you'd like me to prostitute myself for you, would you?" she suggests. "You mustn't look at it that way. One has to take one's chances were one finds them. It's just business. And then there's the revolution that's on the horizon . . . Nothing better than a revolution to boost business for a café." She pretends to accept and swears, by the crucifix above the bed, that she will marry Joseph. Joseph now no longer sees any reason why they should not make love, so they hop into bed. Célestine takes advantage of the situation to get him to talk. A little later, she denounces him to the police, after assembling the necessary evidence to prove without any doubt that he is the murderer. Up to this point, Buñuel remains very faithful to Mirbeau, but he draws only on those passages in the book that interest him. Paradoxically enough, he composes an extremely personal scenario from elements chosen at random from the original, in the best tradition of surrealist paper cut-outs and *collages*. From here on, Buñuel follows the novel less faithfully in order to express its pamphleteering qualities more visually.

The Rabour-Monteils have a neighbour, a retired commander called Mauger, who spends his time pottering about his garden and squabbling about the party wall, branches that overhang the fence, and all the other sorts of things that cantankerous property-owners thrive on. Monteil accuses him of having tipped some rubbish on a piece of track belonging to the Rabour-Monteils, and of having chosen to do so the day of the funeral of grandfather Rabour, who died clutching a boot to his cheek (and who was known in the area as The Cobbler). Mauger did in fact tip a whole wheelbarrowful of old junk on the Monteils' land. The dispute grows increasingly acrimonious, and ends up with them before a magistrate who confronts their two versions of the affair. Mauger gets on his high horse. The magistrate notices the stripes and decorations he has won in battle. "On my word of honour as a soldier, I swear that I never tipped any rubbish on his land," declares Mauger, without batting an eyelid. The magistrate be-

Jeanne Moreau with Buñuel on the set of DIARY OF A CHAMBERMAID

lieves him: "May I point out, Monsieur Monteil, that it is highly unlikely that a stout-hearted soldier like this, an officer who won all his promotions on the field of battle, would take pleasure in throwing old hats into your garden like . . . like a child."

Mauger lives with Rose, a motherly housekeeper who admires him enormously and goes around sighing: "What a child!" But he has designs on Célestine. He kicks out Rose and marries Célestine. She has won: at last it is her turn to have servants. This idea of Buñuel's is, I think, much more forceful than Renoir's (where she runs off with the son who is disgusted by his milieu) and even than Mirbeau's (where she marries Joseph, who gets his café in Cherbourg, and writes on the last page of her diary: "Joseph holds me, possesses me like a demon. And I'm happy to be with him . . . I feel that I will do all he wants me to do, and that I will go wherever he tells me to go . . . even if this means committing a crime.").[32]

Meanwhile Joseph's political connections have turned out to be extremely effective. It was impossible to prove his guilt, so he is now an innocent man. We see him in Cherbourg, in front of his café, "A l'Armée Française." His wife, a vulgarly sexy woman, is busy behind the counter. Joseph is standing among the bystanders, contentedly watching a procession organised by his friends go by. The calico banners they are carrying read: "Down with the Republic," "Herriot to the stake," and "Keep France French." They insult a few immigrants and chant: "Long live Chiappe!" People are hawking "L'Action Française." Several people buy copies, including Joseph. He is beaming with happiness. France's greatest hour, the hour of renovation, restoration and national revolution, is just around the corner.

The procession disappears, and the sounds of "Vive Chiappe!" can still be heard. On a wall, to the left of the shop, there is a poster for a brand of apéritif called Picon. The framing leaves out the letters Pi, so that only *con* remains (*con* in French is a far from gentle insult). This, unless it is the freak product of the projection I saw, is Buñuel's wry way of cocking a snoop at the police commissioner who was the idol of *petits bourgeois* right-wing fanatics.

If I have described what may seem like rather too many anecdotal details instead of discussing the style of the direction, which in the case of this film was dismissed as dull and old-fashioned, it is because the form is conditioned by the content and because both the story Buñuel tells and his way of telling it broke clean away from everything that was thought to be cinematically "in" by high-brow Parisian filmgoers. Everyone, from film-makers to journalists, PR-men, and producers, had got deliriously stoned on a cheap brand of liquor known as *"la Nouvelle Vague"* just at the time *The Diary of a Chambermaid* was released. It is a film, like several others directed by Buñuel, that is pejoratively classified as "minor," which would imply that it is worthy of being judged alongside the countless other "minor" run-of-the-mill films by other directors which sink rapidly into oblivion. This is really most unfair. *The Diary of a Chambermaid* is an unequivocal statement, a warning, a political thesis, and a settling of accounts where Buñuel, with his customary humanism, creates the familiar dialectic of freedom, revolt and love. It stands like a lighthouse amidst the ink-black night of the French cinema. And I hope this will never be forgotten by the so-called film-lovers who blindly acclaim the tiniest, most footling piece of cinematic micturition.

Faith, Dogma and Heresy

On his return to Mexico after shooting *The Diary of a Chambermaid*, Buñuel prepared a scenario, whose central character, Simon, was based on Simeon Stylites, a saint who lived in Syria from 390 to 459 A.D., and who took a vow never to leave the top of a pillar; he in fact spent the last thirty-seven years of his life perched in the air. Then Buñuel went about shooting the film, in spite of the shoestring budget imposed by his producer. One day during the shooting, Buñuel jokingly regretted the production's financial limitations, and said he had wanted to be able to put up an even higher, and unfortunately more expensive, pillar because he felt the character could have got the message across more efficiently by being farther from the earth and closer to the skies! This is, in fact, the way Simon reasons, in all seriousness, at the beginning of the story: he abandons one pillar which is about eighteen feet high, and goes and perches on top of another one, at least thirty feet high, which has sculpted capitals and has been presented to

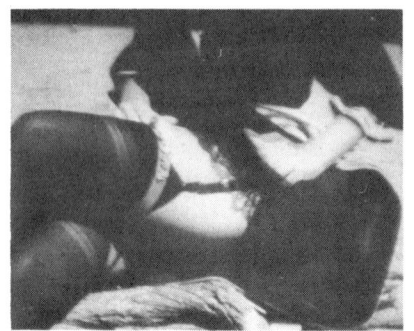 

SIMON OF THE DESERT: Silvia Pinal (left) tries to tempt Simon, and the Monk (right) expostulates fiercely

him by a merchant called Praxedes Mateo. The transfer is an occasion for a little ceremony, including intoned prayers and an officiating bishop: "It has been six years, six weeks and six days now that you have been on top of this pillar, Simon, and have been an example to us all with your asceticism. Move now to another pedestal which is being munificently offered you by the rich Praxedes Mateo. May it please God that you will be able, on your new pillar, to go on being an example to our brothers with your repentance, following as you do in the footsteps of our father Simeon Stylites." The overall meaning of the film is thus suggested right from the start: rich people give the instrument of worship to the man who desires to devote himself utterly to glorifying God, which absolves them from making this sacrifice themselves, eases their consciences, and leaves them the time to deal with worldly affairs. When Simon accepts, he is playing ball with the ruling class; and through his contemplation, which is as barren as it is solitary, he causes the downfall of Christian religion—a religion which, from this point on, suffers from a dualism that often looks like the worst sort of hypocritical double-dealing. It mobilises its doctors to safeguard at all costs the purity of an extraordinarily abstract faith, whence the accumulation of theological scholarship, the defence of dogma, the fight against heresies, the excommunications and burnings at the stake. And yet this same religion takes part in worldly affairs and decides therefore that some sort of compromise has to be worked out.

So there Simon is, cooped up on his disc in the heavens, and having a ding-dong battle with sin without getting his hands dirty. He is like some Nazarin who, discouraged by the wickedness of men and scared by the love of women, still does not know that a peasant girl will give him a pineapple out of friendship and not out of charity, and has decided to devote his whole life to God by seeking refuge in the desert—in other words, in his own proud subjectivity. This emerges very strongly from one of his conversations with his mother.

Mother: Do you sometimes think of me, my son?
Simon: Almost never, Mother. I don't have the time.
Mother: Why are you so proud, my son?
Simon: Proud of my freedom . . .

(*While they speak, there is a shot of Simon, near his mother, picking up a handful of sand and letting it loose in the wind, followed by a shot of Simon on his pillar. He looks down nostalgically.*)

Simon: (*voicing his thoughts*) . . . or of my thraldom, mother?[33]

Attracted as he is by an absolute that is constantly eluding him, he goes through an increasingly intense process of prayer, breast-beating, exaltation and self-mortification in the hope of drawing the mercy of God upon him and his brethren: "We must not yield in our asceticism," he exclaims. "We must bend it like a bow, forget what we are leaving behind, and continue on our flight until we receive the call from heaven . . ."

But Simon's martyrdom does not prevent passions from becoming heated below him on the ground. He is not worried in the slightest about this, as he is convinced that his oblation, which is in the image of that of Christ, will end up by obtaining everyone's redemption. This monumental egoism and self-delusion is not tempered when a monk called Daniel climbs up to Simon on a ladder and attempts to change his mind: "Your disinterestedness is admirable and highly efficacious for your soul. But I fear that, just like your penitence, it is not of much use to mankind." Horror of horrors! Daniel, with his talk of a soul that is of no use unless it is incarnate and, or so he hints, devoted to the struggle of the exploited against the exploiters, sounds like some of our modern fighting priests. Simon gives him the cold shoulder. His main concern is with breaking his records of resistance to pain and starvation, and with seeing if he can keep going on less water and fewer lettuce leaves. In other words, he approaches his apostolate in the same way as a runner approaches a race in a crowded stadium.

★ ★ ★

Jacques Goimard, in the best article I have seen on Buñuel's film,[34] has this to say about Simon's model, Simeon Stylites: "He is not, like Saint Anthony, an outcast (even a voluntary one), or the hero of a solitary struggle with the devil. He is ready to take on any bets; he is an Olympic champion in asceticism, a fanatical idol who lived at the time when Christianity was triumphant. He worships prowess, and is interested only in proving that he can go one better than anyone else (in a period when this was less than easy). The monks saw him as an unfair competitor, and the people as a marvel."

Thousands flock from the depths of the country to ask Simon to intercede on their behalf with the good and just God—in other, more prosaic words, they ask for his help in solving the insoluble problems caused by the so-called pitiless Fates. Simon works miracles. When he restores the hands of a man with a family who had had them cut off after committing a theft, he will again be able to work on the farm (which is beneficial for him, but tiring!). His first act after being miraculously healed is to slap his daughter because she is getting on his nerves.

Later on, Simon finds himself left alone. The monks and countrymen have returned to their homes and resumed work. Because he now no longer needs to satisfy demands for miracles or play to the gallery, Simon becomes more introspective. He struggles with himself. He tries to exorcise his innermost fantasies, and begins to see evil everywhere, particularly in the pleasures of the flesh: woman becomes Satan's henchwoman. Slowly he lapses into madness. The more he tries to consolidate his faith in God, the more accentuated his madness and the hypertrophy of his Ego becomes. The rolling of the same drums of Calanda that resounded in *L'Age d'Or* and *Nazarin* adds a nice ironic, derisive touch to this strange spiritual odyssey which, as becomes clearer from this point on, is a categorical condemnation of the dualism that Christianity establishes between body and soul via the symbolism of man's Fall.

Daniel was right to say that a soul floating in the skies was useless and to accuse a religion that makes people prefer heaven to earth. But he did not go far enough. It is a mistake to attack a perverted form of Christianity and then, through *aggiornamento*, to advocate a more human and more committed version of it. It is Christianity itself, as an ideology and as a religion, which should be unmasked because it crushes the men who believe in it, and reveals a mystery to them in order better to prevent them from attaining it.

Satan whisks Simon away and plonks him in a Greenwich Village night club, where he looks like just another beatnik. He still dreams of an ideal Good and an abstract Evil in a society which, in his eyes, is doomed to an apocalypse. If in New York Simon remains true to his former self on the pillar, he will move in hippy circles or become a brilliant left-wing intellectual—a waste of a fine soul. Or else, if he turns his back on God and the Devil, loves women instead of fearing them, and frees himself from the stupid notion of sin, he will work just like his fellow men, side by side with the outcasts of fortune, not necessarily replacing Christ by the Revolution or God by the end of History, but simply being aware of the fact that all individual or collective social situations are closely bound up with a particular moment in the class struggle.

This forty-five minute film, which ends with an unexpected flourish because money ran out, is in my opinion one of Buñuel's finest, most elusive, funniest and at the same time serious works. It is also a marvellous kind of overture to *La Voie lactée*, which illustrates in more detail one of its themes—the foundation of dogma, the derivation of heresies, and consequently the running battle engaged by the upholders of dogma against the heretics with a view to preserving their patrimony, and inculcating respect for their property in order to check the march of progress more efficiently.

In *L'Age d'Or,* Buñuel's Ur-film to which it is difficult not to return regularly, there is a low shot of the feet of two people getting out of a posh car and going into the house for the fashionable party that is being held by Lya Lys's parents. The extremely solicitous chauffeur takes a monstrance out of the car and ceremoniously places it on the kerb as though he were carrying out an important rite. This religious object, once removed from its usual context, assumes a strange presence as it sits on the pavement.

This brief scene is a fairly classical example of the surrealist method of destroying the utilitarian relationship that objects have *vis-à-vis* mankind and revealing the latent absurdity (and poetry) of these objects, as well as of the world of men. The functional purpose of a wide variety of instruments can in this way be transferred to a deliberately unlikely context, creating not only a feeling of incongruity or of being out of their element but also a different, new reality of a purely poetic nature.

This was part at least of Marcel Duchamp's aim in exhibiting a urinal or a bottle-rack, in their original state, in an art gallery. Picasso's bull's head, achieved with a bicycle saddle topped by handlebars, is the result of a similar sort of approach. And in Max Ernst's collages, Magritte's paintings, or in the poems of Jacques Prévert or Benjamin Péret, there is always the same desire to set up a system of nonsensical meanings whose absolute magic truth is intended to show that the incontestability of the assumptions lying behind our apparent rationality is only relative.

This free approach, which consists of bringing together the most dissimilar objects and images in the figurative unity of a disturbing combination, is to be found throughout Buñuel's work. But in *La Voie lactée* it takes on a very particular quality. The director, in the simplest, most casual way, juxtaposes not a monstrance and a pavement, but holy texts, philosophical tirades about God or

L'AGE D'OR: the monstrance that greets Lya Lys on the pavement

Christ, and everyday phrases set in a modern context. The fundamental declarations that define dogma answer the heretics' professions of faith, and vice versa.

In the course of this interminable exchange, the truth constantly changes sides. Each protagonist is convinced that he alone is in the right. But the truth as decreed by the ecclesiastical authorities —an unassailable truth because it was engendered by the divine word—inevitably ends up by having recourse to temporal powers in order to impose itself. Priest and policeman take it upon themselves to apply it; and on occasions, in order to enforce the laws of love and charity, the civil and religious powers that be (whose minions they are) do not shrink from legalising hatred and torture simply because the moral status quo is in danger. Century after century, the Inquisition keeps open a watchful eye, organises burnings at the stake and witch-hunts, and fills lunatic asylums (all this in the name of Christ—but it could equally well be in the name of Lenin). This of course causes a good deal of bitter discussion, because everyone interprets the Scriptures (or Marx, for that matter) in his own way, and because proof of the existence of God (or of the Communist society that is to come) can only be a subjective decision.

This is a vicious circle that cannot be broken. But it provides plenty of food for thought for the doctrinaire pundits who think that their metaphysical gymnastics are attended by the grace of God. They skirmish like the Jesuit and the Jansenist in *La Voie lactée*, happy after their duel to go back to their occupations with the certitude that they have made a great impression on the people (who were more than delighted). One should remember the young monk's question to the Inquisitor:

The young monk: Something is worrying me.
The Inquisitor: Go ahead.
The young monk: I can't help wondering whether it might not

A genial grouping in LA VOIE LACTEE

	be against the will of the Holy Spirit to burn heretics.
The Inquisitor:	(*somewhat surprised*) But it is the justice of *men* that punishes them. It's the secular arm! The heretics aren't punished because they are heretics but because of their rebellious and dangerous behaviour in public.
The young monk:	But then people whose brothers have been burnt will burn others, and so on. (*In a low voice.*) They are bound in their turn to be in possession of the truth . . . What point can there have been in all those millions of deaths?[35]

Integrism comes to be seen as an end in itself. Discipline is preferred to hair-splitting. Bishops shrink from nothing in their desire to convert, condemn, or even destroy those who do not share their belief, which they believe to have been directly handed down to them from on high. They talk threateningly of the Devil and of Hell, but when that is not enough to produce the desired effect they are more than willing to strike terror into people's hearts and minds by saying that they are possessed by the Devil, all in order to preserve the privileges of those who believe in God because, financially, they have something to gain from doing so.

Buñuel intentionally hops back and forth from dogmatic statements and the heresies they caused, smoothly runs together passages from the Bible and quotations from de Sade ("Ah! If your God does exist, then how I hate him!"), and makes a *maître d'hôtel*, a waiter and some bourgeois customers conduct a discourse on the Trinity while at the same time discussing the menu. He also combines events that happen totally by chance with tongue-in-cheek reminders of the miracles described in catechism classes, and spices sequences whose piety would delight Billy Graham with such realistic touches as Christ's question, in breathless tones: "What's the time?" In so doing, Buñuel ruthlessly debunks the whole concept of religious meditation and makes theology look like one enormous hoax clothed in mumbo-jumbo. His documentary description of the heresies brings out all that is unjustifiable in the body of dogma: the sole justification of this dogma is its struggle against a lie which, with a good deal of effrontery, it itself sets up as a lie which should be struggled against.

As the film goes on, Buñuel's demolition of Catholicism becomes more and more devastating: with his derision, irony, humour and geniality he dynamites a spiritual edifice that is little more than a mirage, and demonstrates that when man's nature and condition is looked at in a certain fraternal way dogma is suddenly seen to be the worst heresy of all. This delightfully anti-Christian attitude towards life, far from destroying any sense of mystery, thrives on it.

The two pilgrims of *La Voie lactée,* in the best tradition of the picaresque novel, enjoy the delights of a carefully planned journey (through woods and fields, along motorways, and from one hotel to another) in combination with a number of unexpected encounters; and their message is that respect for your neighbour is a question of feeling rather than the result of doctrinal analysis of the Sacrament or long-winded discussions about the sex of angels.

They leave Paris, meeting on their way a stranger in a black cape and a dwarf who releases a dove (the Father, the Son and the Holy Spirit). Their aim is to reach Santiago de Compostela either on foot or through hitch-hiking. But the journey of these two tramps, who are called Pierre and Jean, does not take place solely in space: it also takes place in time, and they witness a series of scenes from various periods in history, from Christ to the heretics. One morning, for instance, the Virgin Mary turns towards Jesus just as he picks up his razor and says: "Don't shave it off, my son. You look much better with a beard."

A little later, we see a mad priest who has escaped from a neighbouring asylum discussing the Eucharist with a sceptical police inspector in a country inn. The concluding remark of the innkeeper is reminiscent of what Nazarin says when he talks about the same subject with Andara:

Andara: And God is everywhere, isn't he?

Don Nazario: Yes, everywhere.

Andara: He is also in pancakes. (*Nazarin nods*). So when one eats pancakes, it's as though one were receiving Holy Communion, isn't it?

Don Nazario: No, my child. When the priest consecrates the host, the Lord comes down into the host with his whole Being, just as you, for instance, might be contained in a room . . .

The police inspector: Anyway you'll never convince me that

> the body of Christ can be enclosed in a piece of bread!
>
> The priest: You should watch what you say. The body of Christ is not *enclosed* in the bread. Through the sacrament of the Eucharist, the host *becomes* the body of Christ. Whether you like it or not, it is a case of transubstantiation, which is something completely different.
>
> The commissioner: I'm quite willing to believe that, but I must admit I don't understand. It's all a bit beyond me.
>
> The priest: The host *is* Christ's body, it's as simple as that. And you mustn't get it into your head that it is a representation, or a symbol if you like, of the body of our Lord. That's what the Albigenses believed, and the Calvinists, of course. And others too. But it's an extremely serious fallacy!
>
> The inn-keeper: The way I see it, the body of Christ is contained within the host just as a hare is contained with a *pâté*.

The film then moves on from the Eucharist, and deals in much the same tone with the questions raised by Christ's double nature, the trinity, divine grace, free will, the origins of evil, the assumption of the Virgin, and so on.

We next find ourselves in a religious boarding school for girls, the Institut Lamartine, on the day of the spring festival; during a picnic, the girls act out an edifying little scene that is accompanied by a recitative ("If someone says it's allowed . . ." "May he be cursed!"), and Jean has a dream. He sees a detachment of anarchists, carrying black flags and red flags and marching briskly towards a wall, against which they place the Pope, all dressed in white, and shoot him. The man sitting next to Jean, the father of one of the girls, hears a shot:

> The father: What was that? Is there a shooting range around here?
>
> Jean: No . . . no, it was just me. I imagined that the

> Pope was being shot.
>
> The father: What?! Oh, don't worry. A lot of things may happen, but the Pope shot—quite impossible!

I cannot possibly quote all the allusions and theories and all the encounters that occur during Pierre and Jean's historical sightseeing and theological peregrinations, but they include Origen, Saint Basil, Saint John Chrysostom, Marcion, the monophysites, Nestorius, Photinus, Cleobulus, Priscillian bishop of Avila, the Jansenist convulsionaries, the Adamists, the Nicolists, the Virgin Mary, and Christ making some of his better-known speeches, particularly at the wedding feast of Cana.

After multiple adventures, both mundane and supernatural, our two pilgrims reach the end of their journey. The prostitute, mentioned at the beginning of the film by the stranger in a black cape, inveigles them into some bushes, while Jesus, accompanied by his disciples, arrives on the scene looking extremely irritated. Two blind men ask him to restore their sight. Our Lord rubs their eyelids with a bit of earth and spits in their eyes. They are able to see. The film ends with an indefinably lyrical sequence of enormous brio, where we see the feet of Christ and his disciples striding through the grass with the determined step of people who know where they are going. The camera then moves back a little and follows the feet of the two blind men who have been miraculously healed. No one has any difficulty in crossing a small ditch, except the two blind men who prod the ground with their sticks and fail to get across. This ending is as ambiguous as the whole film, even though there are people who think it can be interpreted as meaning that there is no point in regaining the use of one's eyes if one is determined to remain spiritually blind, and that consequently the only miracles are those we work on ourselves; or again that in order to accompany Christ in the true sense of the word one must not let oneself lag behind by him. I should also mention that a little earlier in the film a minor character, in a hotel room, says: "My hatred of science, and my horror of technology, will finally bring me round to this absurd belief in God," and that some people have claimed he is Buñuel's own mouthpiece. Nothing could be further from the truth. Buñuel's only mouthpiece, if he has one, is the film as a whole. He adopts no clearcut position in any of the discussions and refuses to come down on anybody's side—which is something that even his admirers have held against him. They are disappointed because he does not deliver the blanket condemnation they expected of him. This only goes to show how little they have understood this film, or any other film by Buñuel for that matter. Buñuel is no inquisitor, a role he finds repugnant. But what he also finds repugnant is the idea that a truth should or can be preached *ex cathedra,* and then rammed home by soldiers, judges or executioners. It can only be experienced and verified constantly according to the humanist transcendency that it causes.

La Voie lactée is basically a comedy. It is a light-hearted film that is sacrilegious without ever aiming to shock in a facile, superficial way; and it calls for a return to conscious atheism and to an individual autonomy that is closely bound up with the desire for collective freedom and with a non-theoretical, concrete struggle against intellectual imperialism. The poetry of Buñuel, from *L'Age d'Or* to *Tristana,* always obeys Lautréamont's ideal of practical truth. It can be interpreted on several levels; and the spectator, depending on his background, his doubts, his convictions and his way of thinking, will find this interpretation rewarding to a varying degree. But he will always find it enthralling.

The Invisible and the Visible

When one remembers that an extraordinary wide range of differing opinions were voiced about *Belle de jour,* that the selection committee of the Cannes Festival did not see fit to include it in the competition, and that most critics, even after it received the Grand Prix at the Venice Film Festival in 1967, pigeonholed it as one of the director's minor works, one is naturally tempted to assume that the general public might have some difficulty in making up their mind about the film. This is not because Buñuel either overestimates them or tries to mystify them, but quite simply because they have been conditioned by third-rate forms of theatrical, cinematic, literary and above all televised entertainment, because their emotional powers have become atrophied and are as obedient as those of Pavlov's dog, and because their sensibilities have been drastically blunted by contact with a functionarised world that hides its true colours beneath the gaudy trappings of fashion, advertising, and intellectual snobbery put over by the mass media.

Such spectators are guided by a perfunctory brand of rationalism that is puffed up to be the height of intelligence, and feel at home in the glossy world in which the photographer in *Blow-Up* moves before he comes face to face with mystery. So on the whole they tend to scour Buñuel's labyrinth of significance in search of a continuity that they find familiar, and insist on trying to fathom the behaviour of the central character by referring to the psychological and other similarly regimented semantic keys offered by our society. When thus pursued, the significance of the film of course eludes them. And in order to reassure themselves they stick a label on it: portrait of a masochist, for example, or the fantasies of frustration, or a display of imaginary vices, or the picturesque exploitation of a wide range of sexual perversions—as though Buñuel had bothered, under the cunning pretext of making a dream film, to try and disguise some sort of smutty story of the type that

165

BELLE DE JOUR: Séverine is dragged away to her punishment by "two liveried brutes"

forms the staple diet of vaudeville or boulevard comedy audiences.

In fact *Belle de jour* could not be further removed from that sort of commercial approach. It is neither a novel of manners nor a seedy piece of morbid titillation. It is first and foremost a poem. Anyone who tries to translate the film into clear prosaic terms will be completely non-plussed. The deeper meaning of the story was not first carefully worked out by Buñuel, and then transmogrified into a cryptic language and laced with porn to keep the public's interest up; it arises, on the contrary, from the breadth of a theme that obeys the rhythm and inspiration of automatic writing. *Belle de jour* is a kind of kaleidoscope whose changing patterns can only be apprehended in a magical, indefinable way and vary according to the mood and predisposition of the viewer. A chain of events which seems to be real makes another chain of events seem to be

BELLE DE JOUR: Michel Piccoli and Catherine Deneuve

part of a dream; then suddenly the tables are turned, the second chain becoming real, and the first a mere memory or hallucination. Past, present, future, memory, imagination, and immediate sensation all dovetail together and sometimes seem to fuse without really doing so. One is reminded of the popular illustrations entitled "Where is the hunter?" (he is lurking in a tangle of foliage), or of Arcimboldi's portraits, where one is quite unable to say whether one perceives simultaneously or successively the fruit, vegetables, fish, and the human face they constitute. Similarly in *Belle de jour,* what seems to be an enigma suddenly becomes clear (and turns what had seemed to be clear into an enigma); and the spectator begins to wonder whether the real enigma may not be himself.

It is well known that the study of the vocabulary of a poem, its grammatical analysis and its semantic explanation do not alone enable one to grasp its marvellous, elusive beauty. In this line by André Breton, for instance: "My wife with her sexual organs of sea-weed and old sweets," the subterranean reality that emerges from these words results from an alchemy of words; the lexicological substance that forms the basis of this phrase has undergone a change that lies beyond the bounds of any linguistic science, whether it be structuralist or otherwise. *Belle de jour,* like all Buñuel's films, results from precisely this process. Its sequences form a kinetic architecture in which the signs of fiction are inseparable from the materiality of the radiant presence that informs them. If this presence works its magic on the spectator, the whole film comes across as the revelation of a wonderful truth both for the eyes and the mind; if not, all that is left is decorativeness plus a vague reminder, as far as the plot is concerned, of the second-rate novel by Joseph Kessel that Buñuel used as his point of departure.

The film's centre of gravity lies in the relationship between Séverine and her charming young husband, Pierre, who is a surgeon. The opening sequence shows them going up the drive of a *château* in a horse-drawn carriage against the background of russet leaves and autumnal light that accompanies the whole film. The two liveried brutes who are driving the carriage bring their pair of horses to a halt. On Pierre's instructions, they grab Séverine, drag her out of the carriage in much the same way as Arcibaldo drags his tailor's dummy towards the pottery kiln, gag her, tie her to a branch, and whip her in front of Pierre, who then walks away indifferently, remarking: "She is all yours." The very next moment, we see Séverine in her bedroom with her husband, who asks her: "What are you thinking about?" "About you," she replies. Then she remembers a meeting with the rakish Husson at a skiing resort, where she was fascinated by his glances and his sarcastic pronouncements such as: "One never gets bored in a bar. It's not the same as in church, where one is all alone with one's soul."

When Séverine gets back to Paris, Husson's mistress tells her that one of their women friends, who has the reputation of being a paragon of refined upper-class elegance, in fact prostitutes herself. This discovery surprises and intrigues Séverine; her imagination is stimulated and for some reason unknown to her she gets the urge to do the same thing. She keeps on thinking about it, and when she gets home commits a series of *actes manqués,* knocking over a vase of flowers and smashing a bottle of scent by mistake. Now the voluptuous prisoner of her own obsessions, she remembers that when she was a little girl a plumber who had come to her parents' flat to repair some piping had caressed her: when her mother called her, she did not answer, but let him go on . . .

After casually finding out from her husband what goes on in brothels, she gets Husson to give her the address of a *maison de rendezvous.* She decides to pay a visit there. As she goes up the stairs, feeling a mixture of fear and fascination, she remembers her first Holy Communion as a girl of fourteen, when she refused to take the host offered her by the priest. Séverine's two childhood memories suggest one of the possible origins of the ambivalence of her adult behaviour. She thirsts for sensual pleasure, but her husband does not satisfy her; so she seeks compensation through her imagination. The refusal of the host may indicate a vague sense of guilt (after being caressed by the plumber, our little Christian feels herself to be unclean) as well as a desire not to accept the yoke of religion. Unsatisfied, traumatised, and determined to experience every kind of sensual enjoyment, she tends towards masochism.

She attempts, without success, to forget her project by going to visit her husband at the hospital, but he is too involved with professional problems to be concerned with those of his wife. So she returns to the brothel, which is run by a certain Madame Anaïs. As it is decided that she will work only in the afternoons, she is nicknamed Belle de jour (the name of a convolvulus whose flowers only open during the daytime). She is introduced to her first client, Monsieur Adolphe, a lewd, joky, podgy industrialist. When she gets home that evening after her first "short time," Séverine is not quite sure whether to feel disgusted or happy at having taken the plunge. By pretending not to feel very well, she avoids the need to come into contact with Pierre and is able to indulge in the solitary, bittersweet pleasure of her exhilarating secret. She burns her underwear in the fireplace (whether to exorcise her defilement or because she has decided to stop wearing them, one is not quite sure). Then she dreams she is in the Camargue in the midst of a herd of bulls. We are told by Husson that they all have names, like cats. Some of them are called Remorse, and others Expiation. Husson, egged on by her husband, flings handfuls of mud in her face.

The brothel in BELLE DE JOUR

For a whole week, she is afraid to return to Madame Anaïs's establishment. But her desire proves too strong for her, and she decides to go back. The proprietress forgives her absenteeism, and tells her that a very important client is expected, who will be for her. He arrives carrying a large suitcase. He turns out to be a well-known professor of gynaecology who gets his kicks out of dressing up as a manservant and making his partner play the role of a woman employer who gives him the sharp edge of her tongue because he has not dusted the furniture properly. Looking absurdly pathetic in his striped waistcoat and holding his duster, he falls to his knees and begs forgiveness: "Please Madam, take pity on me and keep me in your service." Séverine is rather disconcerted by her harmless kinky customer, and finds it impossible to keep a straight face while playing the role he needs in order to get himself worked up. Madame Anaïs replaces her by a more experienced colleague and asks her young greenhorn to gen up on things by watching the scene through a voyeur's peephole. Séverine watches the bizarre goings-on, then asks herself: "How can anyone stoop so low?" On another day, she is delivered to the capricious mercies of a huge Korean who has a habit of jingling sleighbells and who shows off a japanned box which, when opened, emits a strange buzzing sound. After a brutal bout of love-making, he leaves the exhausted Séverine in a pleasant swoon among the rumpled sheets. Her next assignment is to go to a country house, where a cynical, vainglorious aristocrat makes her lie naked in a coffin, adorns her with asphodels, and gazes at her for some considerable time before lying down beneath the catafalque—which then shakes to a jerky rhythm. This windswept mansion is reminiscent of Count Zaroff's citadel in *The Most Dangerous Game*, except that here the mastiffs are replaced by cats, which we do not see but can hear cater-wauling. At one of the climaxes of the ritual, the major-domo asks his master: "Shall I let the cats in?" a question which provokes a sharp reprimand. When the onano-necrophiliac ceremony is over,

Séverine is flung out of the *château* like some intruder. She wakes up in bed, beside Pierre, and says to him sincerely: "I love you a little more every day." Then she imagines she is back at the skiing resort: she falls to the ground underneath a table beside Husson, with an envelope that contains asphodel seeds and a broken bottle. "They're writing a letter," remark their friends tersely without taking any interest in them. The table begins to shake just like the coffin in the castle.

Then there is a flurry of new developments in the plot. One of her clients at Anaïs's establishment is a young hood who has just robbed a bank messenger. Marcel is a client with a difference: he wants her all to himself. His affection both disturbs and delights her. She goes for a holiday by the sea with her husband, but at her instigation they cut short their stay and return to Paris. She dreams that Husson and Pierre are fighting a duel, and that she, who has been tied to a tree in order to witness the event, is the one who is killed with a shot through the forehead.

Pierre tells her he wants a child, which does not seem to affect her very much. His way of justifying carnal love with utilitarian ends would seem to accentuate her frigidity in their sexual relationship and heighten her delight in solitary pleasures and voluptuous humiliations. Husson, who is one of Madame Anaïs's former *habitués*, calls in on her one day, discovers Séverine, but refuses to go with her. Marcel gets hold of her address and follows her home; but when he realises that there is no future in their liaison he goes out into the street, lets off his pistol at Pierre and is eventually shot by the police.

Pierre is paralysed, and restricted to a wheelchair. Husson drops in one day and tells Séverine that he is going to spill the beans to her uncomprehending husband: "He thinks you're a paragon of purity. It'll be doing him a service." When he emerges from Pierre's room, Séverine remains quite calm and indifferent. She prepares some drinks on a tray and prepares to get back to her sewing, just

Pierre Clémenti "lets off his pistol at Pierre" in BELLE DE JOUR

like any other neglected bourgeois housewife who has to put up with household chores and routine sex with apparent contentedness. She turns towards Pierre, who is weeping, and who suddenly gets up as though nothing were wrong with him. Cats can be heard yowling and bells jingling. She goes to the window. Instead of the street, there is the drive of the opening sequence, and the carriage goes past, empty. As she stands against this background of russet leaves and autumnal light, we realise that she is at last free and ready to come to grips with life.

Anyone with a smattering of knowledge about surrealist theory will be able to appreciate the hidden beauties of *Belle de jour*. The careless spectator might assume Buñuel's talents as a director to be merely those of a rich man's Jean Delannoy; but when observed attentively the film reveals countless overlapping elements, the most important indication of these being incongruous dialogue and a seething soundtrack. As in *L'Age d'Or,* the sleighbells are the harbingers of wild, violent passion. Buñuel is not a film-maker who needs to resort to the sort of pretentious gimmicks that are influenced by Pop Art or the Nouveau Roman in order to be modern. As in the work of André Delvaux, another film-maker who is a genuine modern poet in his way of breaking down the barriers between dream and reality in order to inject the reality of the dream into the everyday, and as with such painters as Magritte or Balthus, the figurative style remains apparently traditional in order better to stimulate our blunted sensibilities and reveal the latent essence of the behaviour, the things and the world around us and within us.

Buñuel's full maturity once again lends him a cool self-assurance which is not that of someone aiming merely to shock. He also steers clear of all the conventions of cinematic dream sequences, the *clichés* of *avant-garde* films, and even for that matter the use of Freudian symbolism, which does not however prevent his personal emblematic obsessions from being present all through the film—the shoes, the fire in front of which *Belle de jour* repeats Viridiana's movements, the ropes, and the jumble of strange instruments in the professor's suitcase. He deftly inserts brief memories (the plumber who caresses her, the communion she refuses) or little scenes, such as when Madame Anaïs comments on the school work of her maid's little girl, which put the whole descriptive fabric of the film in perspective: Buñuel is then able to give free rein to his fondness for *collage,* humour, preposterous gags, and freaks of chance. Just as, in *Viridiana,* the roistering beggars take up the pose of the figures in Da Vinci's *Last Supper,* the Angelus here triggers off a reference to Millet's famous painting, and the black veil that shrouds Séverine's pearl-white nakedness at the castle comes as a kind of homage to Clovis Trouille. Allusions, visual puns, pastiche, rhetorical dislocation and lyrical purple passages all combine with the classical richness of this love song to take us on a journey into the recesses of a disturbed subconscious and to bring back both the diamond and its matrix.

In several interviews after making *Belle de jour,* Buñuel said that this film would be his last: "It's all over, I'm going to stop," he kept on saying. But occasionally he would also add: "No, I'm not going to shoot any more films. I specialise in enjoying my leisure. From now on, I want to devote myself entirely to the study of this art. But as I'm not a general who has been forcibly retired, as I've given up voluntarily, it's always possible I might have a relapse."

The relapse did indeed come: he made *La Voie lactée* two years later, and followed that up with *Tristana.* In 1969 he managed to set up the production of the latter film in Spain—something that he had failed to do in 1963 because Franco's censors were still mistrustful of Buñuel after the *Viridiana* affair. *Tristana* was adapted from the novel of the same name by Benito Pérez Galdós, the great Spanish writer responsible for the theme of *Nazarin,* and whose novel *Angel Guerra* Buñuel also wanted to adapt for the screen.

The action of *Tristana* is set in Toledo, which according to Monique Morazé is "the symbol, in Galdós's vision of the world, of religious permanence in all its power and nobility." Buñuel slightly up-dates the period of the film, setting it in the early Twenties, in other words the time just before his departure for Paris. So he is thoroughly familiar with his subject, which he treats in an extremely dispassionate manner. He has no axe to grind and produces none of the bravura passages that are expected of him, mistakenly, by those who have a simplistic view of the director. Formally speaking, *Tristana* has a lot in common with *El* and *The Diary of a Chambermaid.* It is a description of the provincial *petite bourgeoisie* which, at first sight anyway, may seem to waver between melodrama and psychological analysis. Against a background of

Catherine Deneuve as TRISTANA

brown and ochre, with the occasional patch of blue, whiteness of washing out to dry, and greenery of a garden, the dominant colour is black (widows' dresses, priests' habits, and policemen's uniforms).

Buñuel evokes the unruffled calm of a small country town—the silent streets, the cosy interiors, the Sunday walks, the housework, the café after Mass, the women busy in the kitchens. He deliberately opts for a style which might, I suppose, be thought to be just a little too slavishly conventional. But Buñuel's coherence and ruthless logic are such that he remains in complete control of the approach he has adopted, and as always in his films realism constantly spills over into poetry. The surreal can be sensed lurking beneath the surface, although it never completely shows its face: with wonderful simplicity, Buñuel uses its implied presence to inject powerful tension into every scene.

Tristana is committed by her dying mother to the charge of an aged liberal gentleman. Unresistingly, and probably with a certain degree of pleasure at first, she is given her sentimental education by him. One day, she visits a church with him, and after spending some time leaning over a marble recumbent figure on a tomb that seems to fascinate her, she is kissed for the first time on the mouth, not far from the altar, by her grizzle-bearded protector. As Don Lope looks like Don Jaime, Viridiana's uncle (they are both played by Fernando Rey), this scene reminds us of *Viridiana,* as well as carrying overtones of Lya Lys being kissed by the bearded conductor in *L'Age d'Or.*

Don Lope inculcates his *protégée* with the principles that guide his own daily life. One afternoon, while they are walking through the town together, they see a thief being chased by a policeman. He scampers round a corner in order to escape his pursuer, who asks Don Lope to tell him which way the rascal has gone. The old man puts the policeman on the wrong track, under the excellent pretext that one should always help the weak and that the police are on the side of the strong.

In several other spheres, Don Lope always displays a keen sense of non-conformism, and particularly concerning anything to do with religion. In this respect he is comparable to Jorge, the architect in *Viridiana.* He is also a typical example of a large number of Spaniards on whom their Catholic education has left a profound stamp and who, in order to prove they still have some desire to emancipate themselves during the period from the end of their adolescence up until the beginning of their old age, are all too willing to adopt a swashbuckling attitude and to stop being practising Catholics, while remaining, in secret, superstitiously attached to their religion. In 1930, there were 20,000 monks, 60,000 nuns, 31,000 priests and almost 5,000 convents and monasteries in Spain, and all important affairs of public or private life went through the Church; but one should not forget that this did not stop two out of every three inhabitants not attending Mass regularly and heartily hating, in many cases, the members of the clergy. Don Lope's anticlericalism, his contempt for work, his repugnance for Christian marriage, its sacred finality and the procreation it involves, stem from the personal moral ethos so common in his fellow-countrymen —an ethos that has managed to free itself of certain taboos but remains the captive of many others connected, for example, with certain social conventions and certain institutions (such as the brothel) which are essential to the maintenance of his situation; it is not as rosy as all that, because he is a bit hard up, but it does ensure him a comfortable feeling of contentedness and a demonstrative attitude of respect from the community.

And yet he fails to see that his generosity is never really much more than verbal, and that above all his criticism of society does not attack the root causes of the evil. "I respect the ten commandments," he says, "except with regard to sexual matters." His servant, Saturna, is there to serve him, and he even asks Tristana to put on his slippers for him! As a result, he is a champion of freedom as far as words are concerned, but when it comes to acts only insofar as they do not threaten his own autonomy, peace of mind, and love of authority, enjoyment and possession. It even may be that he adopts this libertarian stance simply because in the end it guarantees not only his pleasures but his peace of mind. The riot we are shown where mounted police charge some young demonstrators, who defend themselves by throwing stones, does not worry him at all. He simply laments the demise of people's honour, in rather the same way as a bell-ringer might sadly remark that fewer and fewer parishioners believe in God and that, alas, the bells no longer speak directly to the people, who once upon a time used immediately to interpret their message, whether it was the tocsin, the knell, the call to vespers or to high mass, or the full peal at festival time.

While Tristana is moving into his house, Don Lope is very kind and considerate. He shows her some of the family relics and suggests that she take any of them she likes to brighten up her room. To his surprise, she chooses a crucifix. With a mixture of reproof and pride, he remarks drily: "I'm going to be able to get rid of some of your superstitions." But a little later on, while talking to some friends he has invited round for a drink (a ceremony the Spanish call a *"tertulia"*), he refuses to be a second in a duel simply because the two opponents have decided not to fight according to the rules, i.e. until one of them is killed, but to stop the fight as soon as blood is drawn. It is all very well for him to boast of behaving like a progressive, or to say that going into mourning is an uncivilised practice: he is nevertheless, when it comes to certain matters, the unwitting prisoner of a fatuously conservative moral code and of blatantly reactionary ideas. In other words, he haughtily protects his selfishness and the privileges he feels to be the natural due of his class. He refuses either to understand or commit himself to the world. And he manages to keep a clear conscience.

Don Lope asks Tristana to share his bed. Partly intimidated and partly curious, she agrees. But very soon her partner begins to disgust her. At first it is not so much his age that repels her as his lack of imagination in love and his addiction to habit. She is caught up in an inescapable web of monotony, one of the less pleasant symbols of which are his slippers (she ends up by throwing them into a wastepaper basket); and all she dreams of is the open air, gaiety, and youthful vivacity, in just the same way as Séverine dreams of humiliating herself. She meets a handsome young painter called Horacio and falls in love with him. From this moment on, Don Lope's jealousy becomes more and more intense. He baulks at no kind of blackmail ("I'm speaking to you as a father") in order to preserve his marital prerogatives. Tristana leaves him, throwing back into his court some of the excellent principles he had taught her. When the painter leaves Toledo, she

Don Lope is knocked down in the street in TRISTANA

goes with him but refuses to marry him.

Don Lope inherits a fortune from a cantankerous old sister, whom he hated as much as she hated him, and begins to live more comfortably again. He buys back the silver he had sold in order to decorate his house when Tristana first arrived.

Two years later, Tristana returns, a sick woman, and asks Don Lope to take her back into his home. He is only too delighted to accept ("Now she'll never get away"). Tristana contracts a tumour and has to have a leg amputated; although she feels frustrated, she decides to spend the rest of her life under the same roof, manages to persuade Don Lope to give her a church marriage, and devotes herself to charitable work. Her desires are so bottled up and her hankering for an impossible happiness is so intense that she begins to sink into a kind of madness made up of a combination of neurasthenia and an urge for power. She spends hours making herself up in front of a mirror, or furiously hobbling along the corridors of the house on her crutches like a lioness in a cage. An immense hatred springs up between the two. Don Lope lets his former principles go by the board and invites greedy priests to his table, who come to drink Saturna's creamy chocolate beverage, and in the course of conversation poke fun at those countries where "people are perfectly happy to drink nothing but tea" (but who when their host has left them alone for a moment look meaningfully at each other and mutter: "How low he has sunk over the last few months!").

One winter's evening, Don Lope has difficulties in digesting this over-rich drink. He is taken ill, calls Tristana and asks her to telephone for a doctor. She goes into the next room where the telephone is and pretends to do as she is told. Meanwhile, the old man sinks towards a lonely death. Outside it is snowing. Tristana goes and opens the window.

Although the character of Don Lope is the most interesting of the whole film, Tristana's is also extremely intriguing. At the beginning of the film she walks towards the camera (there is considerable depth of composition) dressed in black, accompanied by Saturna, who is also in mourning, and who is coming to visit her son, Saturno. Saturno, who is a pupil in a school for the deaf and dumb, is playing a game of football with his chums. This adolescent, whose mother does not really know what to do with and who later unsuccessfully becomes a blacksmith's apprentice, ends up by becoming, after a succession of paltry jobs, Tristana's servant. His attitude towards her is one of total, fervent admiration. As they are going up a clock-tower together, Tristana, who is still an innocent young girl, leans through a loop-hole to look at the landscape. Saturno surreptitiously lifts up her skirt and gazes at the silky skin of her thigh, right up at the top, between the hem of her stocking and her groin. When they get to the top of the tower, Tristana is much taken by the huge bell and takes hold of its clapper, which looks like an enormous phallus. This is obviously why the bell is replaced in her nightmare by Don Lope's severed head (a double sign of *fellatio* and castration) and why she wakes up in a cold sweat. Don Lope calms her down by saying: "It's a good thing to dream, the dead don't dream." I should perhaps point out that the nightmare may in fact have begun before she goes up the tower, for, as in *Belle de jour*, Buñuel swoops away from reality without any warning. In that case, Saturno's raising of her skirt is a fantasy, a desire on the part of Tristana, who at that point distinctly resembles Séverine.

Unlike her protector, Tristana displays a good deal of imagination and fantasy in day-to-day life. When faced with two precisely similar things—two columns in a cloister, two alleyways, or two chick-peas—she likes to choose and to justify her choice by her sensibility or her capriciousness. This is one of the most charming things about her, and she is right in thinking that Horacio will understand her better than Don Lope. We never know quite what happened between her and the painter. In spite of his kindness and consideration, he disappointed her, just as Pierre disappointed Séverine. Indeed, the only thing that Tristana lacks is the possibility of meeting Husson and getting to know Madame Anaïs's address, where she could become another Belle de jour. Because she is unaware of this way out of things, and because Horacio understands her no better than Don Lope, she prefers, when it comes to the crunch, the old man's financial stability, his assurance, the warm glow of a comfortable life, and, during the misfortune that results in her becoming a cripple, the succour of Catholicism. She takes up the piano again. Buñuel shows her playing, from below the keyboard, with her one foot on the pedal, while the dialogue reminds us that there used to be a one-legged prostitute on Boulevard de la Madeleine who always had plenty of clients;

Opposite: an ageing Tristana is taken in her wheelchair through the town

men found her attractive precisely because of her waddle when she walked and her heron-like posture when at rest. Buñuel shows Tristana hobbling painfully to and fro, a one-legged woman in a bourgeois drawing-room, or lingers a moment on her artificial leg, which she has left on a sofa (one remembers the leg that falls off the tailor's dummy that Arcibaldo drags towards his oven). But it is all treated in an extremely natural way, and never is there any attempt to stress the strangeness of the situation. The camera is placed in such a way that the framing is never baroque, and the smooth rhythm of each sequence is the result of flowing editing that fully respects the extraordinary self-control and nimbleness of the tracking and panning shots.

Pushed by the faithful Saturno in a wheelchair from the house to church or to the park, Tristana gives orders for all manoeuvres with a sharp bark of her voice and a thwack of her stick on the ground. The formerly beautiful young woman has turned into a sour old hag whose thorough nastiness rivals that of Don Lope's deceased sister. She has a talk with the priest. He advises her to get married in order to clear up an ambiguous situation that has gone on too long: "You must get over your feeling of repugnance. Old age does a lot to mollify a man. Already he has agreed to accompany you to the church . . ." So the wedding takes place, with the bride and bridegroom dressed in black, kneeling silently before the altar. The atmosphere is funereal. And it is indeed as though it were a funeral for both of them: they have both scotched the illusions of their youth, their enthusiasm, their desire and their love, simply in order to become the forbidding Christian conjugal entity that has the same basis as Imperial Rome.

This interpretation is both over-explicit and not explicit enough. For it is quite possible to see a number of metaphorical parallels for the spiritual journey undertaken by Don Lope and Tristana: a fable, for instance, about a crippled and choleric Spain, or about a Spain that has slithered from Republican ideals into the worst kind of compromises which herald the return of the monarchy. Or again, to take a highly fashionable linguistic line, one could content oneself with detecting in the film a series of intentionally banal *clichés* which the film-maker, according to one such critic, has used as a basis "to abandon an art of expression and denunciation in favour of an art of nomination,"[36] which does not really get us very much further.

With *Tristana*, a narrative made up of countless little everyday details, Buñuel once again demonstrates the ambiguity of our values and the relativity of our judgements without ever ramming the fact down our throats. He also shows that no genuine revolt can tolerate any kind of compromise and that no passion can survive without constant nourishment: it must devour us at all times. The trouble is that our condition as human beings tends to make us always want our passion to *last;* we want to make it permanent because we are afraid to lose that nugget of gold which we are constantly trying to track down but of which we never find more than a shadow, that nugget which can only be gained if we take the risk of losing it—in other words, ourselves. We are doomed to senile decay; and all that awaits us at the end of the road is death. Weariness can encourage our cowardice and our thirst for thrift. But nothing can ever be permanently secured. The conquests of passion must not be stockpiled because their capital gain is nil. If the price is to be maintained, only the most courageous course must be taken, which is that of putting them constantly at stake according to a responsibility and a faithfulness of which only we, in the last resort, can be the judges: we alone control the metamorphoses of our existence and we alone are the mystery that throws the arch of dialogue between the invisible and the visible.

Footnotes

[1] Jacques Brunius: *En Marge du Cinéma Français*, pp. 137–138. Published by Arcanes, Paris 1954.

[2] André Breton: *L'Amour Fou*, p. 114. Collection Métaphoses. Published by Gallimard, Paris 1937.

[3] J. B. Brunius, op. cit.

[4] Published in *L'Avant-Scène du Cinéma*. Double issue 27–28, Paris, June–July 1963.

[5] Benjamin Péret: preface to *Anthologie de l'Amour Sublime*, p. 64. Published by Albin Michel, Paris 1956.

[6] In *Nuestro Cine* N° 40, Madrid 1965.

[7] *Mon Frère Louis*, in *Positif* N° 42, November 1961.

[8] J. Francisco Aranda: *Luis Buñuel*. Published by Editorial Lumen, Barcelona 1970.

[9] *Cahiers du Cinéma* N° 36, June 1954.

[10] Ibid.

[11] *Ciné-Voyage en Espagne*, by Yvonne Baby, in *Le Monde*, August 13, 1965.

[12] *Passage de Buñuel*, by Jean Duvignaud, in *La Gazette de Lausanne*, February 24, 1962.

[13] Jacques Prévert: *Spectacle*, p. 209. Published by Gallimard, Collection Point du Jour, Paris 1951.

[14] Op. cit.

[15] Op. cit.

[16] Gaston Bachelard: *Lautréamont*, p. 133. Published by José Corti, Paris 1939.

[17] Pierre Mabille: *Thérèse de Lisieux*, p. 43. Published by José Corti, Paris 1937.

[18] Ibid., p. 92.

[19] D.A.F. de Sade: *Dialogue entre un Prêtre et un Moribond*, p. 15. Published by J. J. Pauvert, Paris 1953.

[20] *Buñuel Mexicain*, by Jean Delmas, in *Jeune Cinéma* N° 12, February 1966.

[21] Op. cit.

[22] Maurice Blanchot: *L'Entretien Infini*, p. 473. Published by Gallimard, Paris 1969.

[23] Scenario published by *L'Avant-Scène du Cinéma*, p. 86. N° 89, February 1969.

[24] Op. cit. p. 55.

[25] In *Carré Rouge*, N° 4, January-February 1958, Lausanne.

[26] In *Le Monde*, June 1, 1961

[27] Cf. François Chevassu, in *Image et Son* N° 152, June 1962.

[28] Sigmund Freud: *Jokes and Their Relation to the Unconscious*. Published by Norton, New York 1961.

[29] In *Pour Buñuel*. Published by the Cercle du Cinéma de l'AGET, Toulouse. March 1964.

[30] In *Positif* N° 33, April 1960.

[31] In *Etudes Cinématographiques*, N°s 22–23, Vol. 2. First quarter, 1963.

[32] Octave Mirbeau: *Le Journal d'une Femme de Chambre*, p. 347. Published by Fasquelle, Paris 1964.
[33] In *L'Avant-Scène du Cinéma* Nos 94–95. July–September 1969.
[34] In *Positif* No 108. September 1969.
[35] Op. cit.
[36] In *Quinzaine Littéraire* No 95. Paris, May 16, 1970.

Filmography

(compiled by Derek Elley)

All dates are release dates in countries of origin

Italicised titles in brackets are those under which the film was released in G.B./U.S., and are not necessarily translations.

A. Films as Assistant Director

1926: *Mauprat* (dir.: Jean Epstein; Buñuel makes a brief appearance)

1927: *La Sirène des Tropiques* (dir.: Mario Nalpas, Henri Etiévant)

1928: *La Chute de la maison Usher* (dir.: Jean Epstein)

B. Films as Executive Producer

1935: *Don Quintín, el amargao* (Spain; dir.: Luis Marquina)

1935: *La Hija de Juan Simón* (Spain; dir.: José Luis Sáenz de Heredia)

1936: *¿Quién me quiere a mí?* (Spain; dir.: José Luis Sáenz de Heredia)

1937: *¡Centinela, alerta!* (Spain; dir.: Jean Grémillon)

1937: *España leal en armas/Espagne 37* (documentary; Buñuel was responsible for overall supervision, and the commentary with Pierre Unik)

C. Film-work in other capacities

1933–35: work as translator for Paramount in Paris.

The expression of revolt so common to Buñuel's films is well caught in these two shots from UN CHIEN ANDALOU

1935: work as translator and supervisor on co-productions for Warner Bros. in Spain.
1937: assisted Helen van Dongen on editing of *Spanish Earth* (dir.: Joris Ivens).
1938: supervised documentaries for Museum of Modern Art, New York (e.g. *Aves emigratorias*—dir.; *Tejidos cancerosos*—dir., ed.).
1940: work as translator for M-G-M in U.S.A.
1942: director of documentaries for American Army.
1944–46: work as translator for Warner Bros. in U.S.A.

D. Films as Director

1928: UN CHIEN ANDALOU (France). Produced by Luis Buñuel. *Dir.:* Luis Buñuel. *Ass. dir.:* Pierre Batcheff. *Scr.:* Luis Buñuel, Salvador Dali. *Ph.:* Albert Dubergen. *Art dir.:* Schilzneck. Silent (soundtrack added by Buñuel in 1960, based on records played at the première). *Music:* Beethoven, Wagner (*Tristan und Isolde*), and an Argentinian tango. *Edit.:* Luis Buñuel. 17 mins. CAST: Pierre Batcheff (*Cyclist*), Simone Mareuil (*Girl*), Jaime Miravilles, Salvador Dali (*Priest*), Luis Buñuel (*Man with Razor*). *Première:* 1928, Ursulines Film Studio, Paris.

1930: L'AGE D'OR (France). Produced by Charles Vicomte de Noailles. *Dir.:* Luis Buñuel. *Ass. dirs.:* Jacques Brunius, Claude Heymann. *Scr.:* Luis Buñuel, Salvador Dali. *Ph.:* Albert Dubergen. *Art dir.:* Schilzneck. *Music:* Georges van Parys, Beethoven (*Fifth Symphony*), Wagner (*Forest Murmurs* from *Siegfried; Prelude* and *Death of Tristan* from *Tristan und Isolde*), Mendelssohn (*Fourth*

Modot in L'AGE D'OR

The game-keeper shoots his son in L'AGE D'OR

"Italian" Symphony; Fingal's Cave), Mozart (*Ave Verum*), Debussy (*La Mer est plus belle*), and an anonymous *paso doblé*. *Edit.:* Luis Buñuel. 60 mins.
CAST: Gaston Modot (*Man*), Lya Lys (*Woman*), Max Ernst (*Leader of the Bandits*), Pierre Prévert (*Péman, a Bandit*), Caridad de Laberdesque, Liorens Artryas, Jacques Brunius, José Artigas, Lionel Salem, Pancho Cossio, Valentine Hugo, Marie-Berthe Ernst, Madame Noizet, Simone Cottance, Xaume de Miravilles, Duchange, Ibanez, Pruna.
Première: 28 Oct. 1930, Studio 28 Cinéma, Montmartre, Paris.

1932: LAS HURDES—Tierra sin pan (*Terre sans pain/Land without Bread*) (Spain). Produced by Ramón Acín. *Dir.:* Luis Buñuel.

Ass. dirs.: Pierre Unik, Rafael Sánchez Ventura. *Scr.:* Luis Buñuel. *Ph.:* Eli Lotar. *Music:* Brahms (*Fourth Symphony*). *Edit.:* Luis Buñuel. Commentary by Pierre Unik. 27 mins.

1947: GRAN CASINO (Mexico). Produced by Filmadora Anáhuac, S.A. (Oscar Dancigers). *Dir.:* Luis Buñuel. *Ass. dir.:* Moisés Delgado. *Scr.:* Mauricio Magdaleno, Edmundo Báez, based on a story by Michel Weber. *Ph.:* Jack Draper. *Art dir.:* Javier Torres Torija. *Sound:* Javier Mateos. *Music:* Manuel Esperón. *Edit.:* Gloria Schoemann. 85 mins.
CAST: Libertad Lamarque (*Mercedes Irigoyen*), Jorge Negrete (*Gerardo Ramírez*), Mercedes Barba, Agustín Insunza, Julio Villarreal, Charles Rooner, José Baviera, Francisco Jambrina, Alfonso Bedoya, Bertha Lear.
Start of shooting: 26 Nov. 1946.
Mexican première: 12 Jun. 1947.

1949: EL GRAN CALAVERA (Mexico). Produced by Ultramar Films, S.A. (Oscar Dancigers). *Dir.:* Luis Buñuel. *Ass. dir.:* Moisés Delgado. *Scr.:* Raquel Rojas, Luis Alcoriza, from a comedy by Adolfo Torrado. *Ph.:* Ezequiel Carrasco. *Art dir.:* Luis Moya, Darío Cabanas. *Sound:* Rafael Ruiz Esparza. *Music:* Manuel Esperón. *Edit.:* Carlos Savage. 90 mins.
CAST: Fernando Soler (*Don Ramiro*), Rosario "Charito" Granados, Rubén Rojo, Andrés Soler, Maruja Grifell, Gustavo Rojo, Luis Alcoriza, Antonio Bravo, Francisco Jambrina, Antonio Monsell, Nicolás Rodríguez.
Start of shooting: 9 Jun. 1949.
Mexican première: 25 Nov. 1949.

1950: LOS OLVIDADOS (*The Young and the Damned*) (Mexico). Produced by Ultramar Films, S.A. (Oscar Dancigers). *Dir.:* Luis Buñuel. *Ass. dir.:* Ignacio Villarreal. *Scr.:* Luis Buñuel, Luis Alcoriza. *Ph.:* Gabriel Figueroa. *Art dir.:* Edward Fitzgerald. *Sound:*

José B. Carles. *Music:* Rodolfo Halffter, from themes by Gustavo Pittaluga. *Edit.:* Carlos Savage. 88 mins.
CAST: Alfonso Mejía (*Pedro*), Roberto Cobo (*Jaibo*), Estela Inda (*Marta, Pedro's Mother*), Miguel Inclán (*Don Camelo, the Blind Man*), Efrain Arauz (*"Pockface"*), Mario Ramírez (*"Ojitos"—"Little Eyes"*), Alma Delia Fuentes (*Meche*), Francisco Jambrina (*Reform School Director*), Javier Amezcua (*Julian*), Héctor López Portillo, Salvador Quiros, Víctor Manuel Mendoza, Jesús Navarro, Diana Ochoa, Charles Rooner, Sergio Villarreal, Jorge Pérez.
Start of shooting: 6 Feb. 1950.
Mexican première: 9 Nov. 1950.

1951: SUSANA (Mexico). Produced by Internacional Cinematográfica, S.A. (Oscar Dancigers). *Dir.:* Luis Buñuel. *Ass. dir.:* Ignacio Villarreal. *Scr.:* Jaime Salvador, from a novel by Manuel Reachi.

Attempted strangling in EL. Note the huge bell like the one in TRISTANA

Dial.: Rodolfo Usigli. *Ph.:* José Ortiz Ramos. *Art dir.:* Gunther Gerzso. *Sound:* Nicolás de la Rosa. *Music:* Raúl Lavista. *Edit.:* Jorge Bustos. 82 mins. (sources vary between 78 and 86 mins.)
CAST: Rosita Quintana (*Susana*), Fernando Soler (*Guadalupe, the Father*), Víctor Manuel Mendoza (*Jesús, the Ranchero*), Matilde Palau (*Doña Carmen, the Mother*), María Gentil Arcos (*Feliza, the Old Servant*), Luis López Somoza (*Alberto, the Son*).
Start of shooting: 10 Jul. 1950.
Mexican première: 11 Apr. 1951.

1951: LA HIJA DEL ENGAÑO (Mexico). Produced by Ultramar Films, S.A. (Oscar Dancigers). *Dir.:* Luis Buñuel. *Ass. dir.:* Mario Llorca. *Scr.:* Raquel Rojas, Luis Alcoriza, from "Don Quintín, el amargao" by Carlos Arniches. *Ph.:* José Ortiz Ramos. *Art dir.:* Edward Fitzgerald. *Sound:* Eduardo Arjona. *Music:* Manuel Esperón. *Edit.:* Carlos Savage. 80 mins.
CAST: Fernando Soler (*Don Quintín*), Alicia Caro, Rubén Rojo, Nacho Contra, Fernando Soto, Lily Aclemar.
Start of shooting: 8 Jan. 1951.
Mexican première: 29 Aug. 1951.

1952: SUBIDA AL CIELO (Mexico). Produced by Producciones Isla (Manuel Altolaguirre). *Dir.:* Luis Buñuel. *Ass. dir.:* Jorge López Portillo. *Scr.:* Juan de la Cabada, Manuel Altolaguirre, Luis Buñuel, after a story by Altolaguirre and Manuel Reachi. *Dial.:* Juan de la Cabada. *Ph.:* Alex Phillips. *Art dirs.:* Edward Fitzgerald, José Rodríguez Granada. *Sound:* Eduardo Arjona. *Music:* Gustavo Pittaluga. *Edit.:* Rafael Portillo. 85 mins.
CAST: Lilia Prado (*Raquel*), Carmelita González (*Oliverio's Wife*), Esteban Márquez (*Oliverio*), Manuel Dondé (*Don Eladio, the Deputy*), Roberto Cobo (*Juan*), Luis Acevez Castañeda (*Silvestre, the Chauffeur*), Gilberto González, Beatriz Ramos, Manolo Noriega, Roberto Meyer, Pitouto, Pedro Ibarra, Leonor Gomez, Chel López,

Paz Villegas de Orellana, Silvia Castro, Paula Rendon, Víctor Pérez.
Start of shooting: 6 Aug. 1951.
Mexican première: 26 Jun. 1952.

1952: UNA MUJER SIN AMOR (Mexico). Produced by Internacional Cinematográfica, S.A. (Oscar Dancigers). *Dir.:* Luis Buñuel. *Scr.:* Jaime Salvador, based on the novel "Pierre et Jean" by Guy de Maupassant. *Ph.:* Raúl Martínez Solares. *Art dir.:* Gunther Gerzso. *Music:* Raúl Lavista. *Edit.:* Jorge Bustos.
CAST: Rosario "Charito" Granados (*Rosario*), Julio Villarreal (*Julio*), Tito Junco (*Carlos*), Joaquín Cordero (*Elder Son*), Jaime Calpe Jnr., Elda Peralta, Xavier Loya.
Start of shooting: 16 Apr. 1951.
Mexican première: 31 Jul. 1952.

1953: EL BRUTO (*The Brute*) (Mexico). Produced by Internacional Cinematográfica, S.A. (Oscar Dancigers). *Dir.:* Luis Buñuel. *Ass. dir.:* Ignacio Villarreal. *Scr.:* Luis Buñuel, Luis Alcoriza. *Ph.:* Agustín Jiménez. *Art dir.:* Gunther Gerzso. *Sound:* Javier Mateos. *Music:* Raúl Lavista. *Edit.:* Jorge Bustos. 83 mins.
CAST: Pedro Armendáriz (*Pedro, the Brute*), Katy Jurado (*Paloma*), Rosita Arenas (*Meche*), Andrés Soler (*Cabrera*), Roberto Meyer, Beatriz Ramos, Paco Martínez, Gloria Mestre.
Start of shooting: 3 Mar. 1952.
Mexican première: 5 Feb. 1953.

1953: ÉL (*This Strange Passion*) (Mexico). Produced by Nacional Film (Oscar Dancigers). *Dir.:* Luis Buñuel. *Ass. dir.:* Ignacio Villarreal. *Scr.:* Luis Buñuel, Luis Alcoriza, from the novel "Pensiamentos" by Mercedes Pinto. *Ph.:* Gabriel Figueroa. *Art dir.:* Edward Fitzgerald. *Sound:* José D. Pérez. *Music:* Luis Hernández Bretón. *Edit.:* Carlos Savage. 100 mins. (G.B.: 91 mins.; U.S.: 80 mins.).
CAST: Arturo de Córdova (*Francisco*), Delia Garcés (*Gloria*), Luis Beristáin (*Raúl*), Aurora Walker (*Doña Esperanza*), Carlos

Martínez Baena (*Padre Velasco*), Fernando Casanova (*Beltrán*), Manuel Dondé (*Pablo*), Rafael Banquells (*Ricardo*), José Pidal, Roberto Meyer.
Start of shooting: 24 Nov. 1952.
Mexican première: 9 Jul. 1953.

1954: LA ILUSIÓN VIAJA EN TRANVÍA (Mexico). Produced by Clasa Films Mundiales, S.A. (Armando Orive Alba). *Dir.:* Luis Buñuel. *Ass. dir.:* Ignacio Villarreal. *Scr.:* Mauricio de la Serna, José Revueltas, Juan de la Cabada, Luis Alcoriza, based on a story by Mauricio de la Serna. *Ph.:* Raúl Martínez Solares. *Art dir.:* Edward Fitzgerald. *Sound:* José D. Pérez. *Music:* Luis Hernández Bretón. *Edit.:* Jorge Bustos. 90 mins.
CAST: Lilia Prado (*Lupe*), Carlos Navarro (*Caireles*), Domingo Soler, Fernando Soto (*Tarrajas*), Agustín Isunza (*Pinillos*), Miguel Manzano, Javier de la Parra, Guillermo Bravo Sosa, Felipe Montojo, José Pidal, Felipe Montoya, Diana Ochoa, Víctor Alcocer.
Start of shooting: 28 Sep. 1953.
Mexican première: 18 Jun. 1954.

1954: ABISMOS DE PASIÓN (Mexico). Produced by Tepeyac Producciones, S.A. (Oscar Dancigers, Abelardo Rodríguez). *Dir.:* Luis Buñuel. *Ass. dir.:* Ignacio Villarreal. *Scr.:* Luis Buñuel, Arduino Maiuri, Julio Alejandro de Castro, based on the novel "Wuthering Heights" by Emily Brontë. *Ph.:* Agustín Jiménez. *Art dir.:* Edward Fitzgerald. *Sound:* Eduardo Arjona. *Music:* Wagner (*Tristan und Isolde*), adapted by Raúl Lavista. *Edit.:* Carlos Savage. 90 mins.
CAST: Irasema Dilian (*Katy*), Jorge Mistral (*Alejandro*), Lilia Prado, Ernesto Alonso, Luis Aceves Castañeda, Francisco Reiguera.
Start of shooting: 23 Mar. 1953.
Mexican première: 3 Jul. 1954.

1954: ADVENTURES OF ROBINSON CRUSOE/ROBINSÓN CRUSOE (US/Mexico). Produced by Ultramar Films, S.A. (Henry

F. Ehrlich, Oscar Dancigers). *Dir.:* Luis Buñuel. *Ass. dir.:* Ignacio Villarreal. *Scr.:* Luis Buñuel, Philip A. Roll, from the novel by Daniel Defoe. *Dial.:* Luis Buñuel. *Ph.:* Alex Phillips (Pathécolor). *Art dir.:* Edward Fitzgerald. *Sound:* Javier Mateos. *Music:* Luis Hernández Bretón, Anthony Collins. *Edit.:* Carlos Savage, Alberto Valenzuela. 89 mins.
CAST: Dan O'Herlihy (*Robinson Crusoe/Robinsón Crusoe*), Jaime Fernández (*Friday/Viernes*), Felipe de Alba (*Cpt. Oberzo*), Chel López (*Bosun*), José Chávez and Emilio Garibay (*Mutineers*).
Start of shooting: 14 Jul. 1952.
U.S. première: Jul. 1954; *G.B. première:* Aug. 1954.
Mexican première: 30 Jun. 1955.
Shot simultaneously in two versions, English and Spanish.

1955: EL RÍO Y LA MUERTE (Mexico). Produced by Clasa Films Mundiales, S.A. (Armando Orive Alba). *Dir.:* Luis Buñuel. *Ass. dir.:* Ignacio Villarreal. *Scr.:* Luis Buñuel, Luis Alcoriza, from the novel "Muro Blanco sobre Roca Negra" by Miguel Alvarez Acosta. *Ph.:* Raúl Martínez Solares. *Art dir.:* Edward Fitzgerald, Gunther Gerzso. *Sound:* José D. Pérez. *Music:* Raúl Lavista. *Edit.:* Jorge Bustos. 90 mins.
CAST: Columba Domínguez (*Mercedes*), Miguel Torruco (*Felipe Anguiano*), Joaquín Cordero (*Gerardo Anguiano*), Jaime Fernández (*Rómulo Menchaca*), Víctor Alcocer (*Polo*), Silvia Derbez (*Elsa*), Humberto Almazán (*Crescencio*), Alfredo Varela Jnr. (*Chinelas*), José Elías Moreno, Carlos Martínez Baena, Miguel Manzona, Manuel Dondé, Jorge Arriaga, Roberto Meyer, Chel López, José Munoz.
Start of shooting: 25 Jan. 1954.
Mexican première: 28 Feb. 1955.

1955: ENSAYO DE UN CRIMEN (*The Criminal Life of Archibaldo de La Cruz*) (Mexico). Produced by Alianza Cinematográfica, S.A. (Alfonso Patiño Gómez). *Dir.:* Luis Buñuel. *Ass. dir.:* Luis

Abadie. *Scr.:* Luis Buñuel, Eduardo Ugarte Pages, from the story by Rodolfo Usigli. *Ph.:* Agustín Jiménez. *Art dir.:* Jesús Bracho. *Sound:* Rodolfo Benítez. *Music:* Jorge Pérez Herrera. *Edit.:* Jorge Bustos. 91 mins.
CAST: Ernesto Alonso (*Archibaldo de La Cruz*), Miroslava Stern (*Lavinia*), Rita Macedo (*Patricia*), Ariadna Welter (*Carlota*), Rodolfo Landa, Andrés Palma, Carlos Riquelme, José Maria Linares Rivas, Leonor Llansás, Eva Calvo, Carlos Martínez Baena, Roberto Meyer, Rafael Banquels Jnr.
Start of shooting: 20 Jan. 1955.
Mexican première: 3 Apr. 1955.

1956: CELA S'APPELLE L'AURORE/AMANTI DI DOMANI (France/Italy). Produced by Les Films Marceau, Paris/Laetitia Film, Rome. *Dir.:* Luis Buñuel. *Ass. dirs.:* Marcel Camus, Jacques Deray. *Scr.:* Luis Buñuel, Jean Ferry, from the novel by Emmanuel Robles. *Dial.:* Jean Ferry. *Ph.:* Robert Lefebvre. *Art dir.:* Max Douy. *Sound:* Antoine Petitjean. *Music:* Joseph Kosma. *Edit.:* Marguerite Renoir. 102 mins.
CAST: Georges Marchal (*Dr. Valerio*), Lucia Bosè (*Clara*), Gianni Esposito (*Sandro*), Julien Bertheau (*the Commissioner*), Nelly Borgeaud (*Angela*), Jean-Jacques Delbo (*Gorzone*), Robert Le Fort (*Pietro*), Brigitte Elloy (*Magda*), Henri Nassiet (*Angela's Father*), Gaston Modot (*a Corsican Peasant*), Pascal Mazotti (*Azzopardi*), Simone Paris (*Mme. Gorzon*).
Location filming (*in Corsica and around Nice*): 18 Aug. 1955–14 Oct. 1955.
French première: 9 May 1956; *Italian première:* Autumn 1957.

1956: LA MORT EN CE JARDIN/LA MUERTE EN ESTE JARDÍN (*Evil Eden*) (France/Mexico). Produced by Dismage, Paris (David Mage)/Producciones Teperac, Mexico (Oscar Dancigers). *Dir.:* Luis Buñuel. *Scr.:* Luis Buñuel, Luis Alcoriza, Raymond Queneau, from the story by José-André Lacour. *Dial.:* Raymond Queneau, Gabriel Arout. *Ph.:* Jorge Stahl Jnr. (Eastmancolor). *Art dir.:* Edward Fitzgerald. *Sound:* José D. Pérez. *Music:* Paul Misraki. *Edit.:* Marguerite Renoir. 104 mins. (France/G.B.)/145 mins. (Mexico) (U.S.: 110 mins.).

CAST: Simone Signoret (*Gin*), Georges Marchal (*Chark*), Michel Piccoli (*Father Lisardi*), Michèle Girardon (*Maria, the Mute*), Charles Vanel (*Castin*), Tito Junco (*Chenko, the Skipper*), Luis Aceves Castañeda (*Alberto*), Jorge Martínez de Hoyos (*Captain Ferrero*), Alicia del Lago, Raúl Ramírez (*Alvaro*), Alberto Pedret (*Lieutenant*), Stefani (*First Worker*), Marc Lambert (*Second Worker*).

French première: 21 Sep. 1956; *Mexican première:* 9 Jun. 1960.

1959: NAZARÍN (Mexico). Produced by Manuel Barbachano Ponce. *Exec. prod.:* Federico Amérigo. *Dir.:* Luis Buñuel. *Ass. dir.:* Ignacio Villarreal. *Scr.:* Luis Buñuel, Julio Alejandro, from the novel by Benito Pérez Galdós. *Dial.:* Emilio Carballido. *Ph.:* Gabriel Figueroa. *Art dir.:* Edward Fitzgerald. *Music:* no credit; only drumbeat at end. *Edit.:* Carlos Savage. 94 mins.

CAST: Francisco Rabal (*Nazarín*), Marga López (*Beatriz*), Rita Macedo (*Andara*), Jesús Fernández (*Ujo, the Dwarf*), Ignacio López Tarso (*the "Good Thief"*), Ofelia Guilmain (*Chanfa*), Noé Murayama (*El Pinto*), Luis Aceves Castañeda (*the Murderer*), Rosenda Monteros (*the Dark Girl*), Aurora Molina, Pilar Pellicer, Antonio Bravo, Edmundo Barbero, Raúl Dantés.

Mexican première: 4 Jun. 1959.

1960: LA FIÈVRE MONTE À EL PAO/LOS AMBICIOSOS (*Republic of Sin*) (France/Mexico). Produced by CICC, Cité Films, Indus Films, Terra Films, Cormoran Films, Paris (Raymond Borderie)/Cinematográfica Filmex, S.A. (Mexico). *Prod. man.:* Charles Borderie. *Dir.:* Luis Buñuel. *Ass. dir.:* Ignacio Villarreal. *Scr.:* Luis Buñuel, Luis Alcoriza, Louis Sapin, Charles Dorat, based on the novel by Henri Castillou. *Dial.:* Louis Sapin. *Ph.:* Gabriel Figueroa.

Art dir.: Jorge Fernández. *Sound:* William Robert Sivel. *Music:* Paul Misraki. *Edit.:* James Cuenet, Rafael López Ceballos. 97 mins. (France)/110 mins. (Mexico).

CAST: Gérard Philipe (*Ramón Vásquez*), María Félix (*Inès Vargas*), Jean Servais (*Alejandro Gual*), Miguel Angel Ferriz (*Governor Vargas*), Raúl Dantés (*García*), Domingo Soler (*Professor Gardenas*), Víctor Junco (*Indarte*), Roberto Cañedo (*Olivares*), Tito Junco, Andrés Soler, Luis Aceves Castañeda, Augusto Benedíco.

Start of shooting: 11 May 1959.
French première: 6 Jan. 1960; *Mexican première:* 20 Oct. 1960.

1960: THE YOUNG ONE/LA JOVEN (original English release title: *Island of Shame*) (U.S./Mexico). Produced by George Werker, U.S./Producciones Olmeca, Mexico. *Dir.:* Luis Buñuel. *Ass. dirs.:* Ignacio Villarreal, Juan-Luis Buñuel. *Scr.:* Luis Buñuel, H. B. Addis (Hugo Butler), from the novel "Travellin' Man" by Peter Matthiessen. *Ph.:* Gabriel Figueroa. *Art dir.:* Jesús Bracho. *Sound:* José B. Carles, Galdino Samperio. *Music:* Jesús Zarzoza (song "Sinner Man" sung by Leon Bibb). *Edit.:* Carlos Savage. 95 mins.

CAST: Zachary Scott (*Miller*), Key Meersman (*Evalyn*), Bernie Hamilton (*Travers*), Crahan Denton (*Jackson*), Claudio Brook (*Reverend Fleetwood*).

G.B. premières: Nov. 1960 (London Film Festival); 14 Dec. 1961 (general); *Mexican première:* 4 Aug. 1961.

1961: VIRIDIANA (Spain/Mexico). Produced by Uninci, Films 59, Madrid/Gustavo Alatriste, Mexico. *Exec. prod.:* Ricardo Munoz Suay. *Dir.:* Luis Buñuel. *Ass. dirs.:* Juan-Luis Buñuel, J. Pujol. *Scr.:* Luis Buñuel, Julio Alejandro. *Ph.:* José F. Aguayo. *Art dir.:* Francisco Canet. *Music:* Handel (*Messiah*), Mozart (*Requiem*). *Music dir.:* Gustavo Pitaluga. *Edit.:* Pedro del Rey. 90 mins.

CAST: Silvia Pinal (*Viridiana*), Fernando Rey (*Don Jaime*), Francisco Rabal (*Jorge, his Son*), Margarita Lozano (*Ramona*), Victoria

Zinny (*Lucía*), Teresa Rabal (*Rita*), and José Calvo, Joaquín Roa, Luis Heredia, José Manuel Martín, Dolores Gaos, Juan García Tiendra, Maruja Isbert, Joaquín Mayol, Palmira Guerra, Sergio Mendizábal, Milagros Tomás, Alicia Jorge Barriga (*the Beggars*). *Première:* 17 May 1961 (Cannes Film Festival).

After completion the film was banned in Spain and copies confiscated. Some had already left for France, however, and the *première* was consequently at Cannes.

1962: EL ÁNGEL EXTERMINADOR (*The Exterminating Angel*) (Mexico). Produced by Uninci, Films 59 (Gustavo Alatriste). *Dir.:* Luis Buñuel. *Ass. dir.:* Ignacio Villarreal. *Scr.:* Luis Buñuel, from a scenario "Los Náufragos de la calle de la Providencia" by Buñuel and Luis Alcoriza, suggested by the unpublished play "Los Náufragos" by José Bergamín (*see Section E*). *Dial.:* Luis Buñuel. *Ph.:* Gabriel Figueroa. *Art dir.:* Jesús Bracho. *Sound:* José B. Carles. *Music:* Scarlatti, a sonata by Paradisi, various *Te Deums*. *Edit.:* Carlos Savage Jnr. 95 mins.

CAST: Silvia Pinal (*Leticia, the "Valkyrie"*), Enrique Rambal (*Nobile*), Jacqueline Andere (*Señora Alicia Roc*), José Baviera (*Leandro*), Augusto Benedico (*the Doctor*), Luis Beristáin (*Christián*), Antonio Bravo (*Russell*), Claudio Brook (*Majordomo*), César del Campo (*the Colonel*), Rosa Elena Durgel (*Silvia*), Lucy Gallardo (*Lucía, Nobile's Wife*), Enrique García Álvarez (*Señor Roc*), Ofelia Guilmain (*Juana Ávila*), Nadia Haro Oliva (*Ana Maynar*), Tito Junco (*Raúl*), Xavier Loya (*Francisco Ávila*), Xavier Massé (*Eduardo*), Ángel Merino (*Lucas, the Waiter*), Ofelia Montesco (*Beatriz, Eduardo's Fiancée*), Patricia Morán (*Rita, Christián's Wife*), Patricia de Morelos (*Blanca*), Bertha Moss (*Leonora*).

Mexican première: 8 May 1962.

1964: LE JOURNAL D'UNE FEMME DE CHAMBRE (*Diary of a Chambermaid*) (France/Italy). Produced by Spéva Films, Ciné-

Alliance, Filmsonor, Paris/Dear Films, Rome. *Exec. prod.:* Henri Baum. *Dir.:* Luis Buñuel. *Scr.:* Luis Buñuel, Jean-Claude Carrière, from the novel by Octave Mirbeau. *Ph.:* Roger Fellous (Franscope). *Art dir.:* Georges Wakhevitch. *Sound:* Antoine Petitjean. *Music:* none. *Edit.:* Louisette Hautecoeur. 98 mins.
CAST: Jeanne Moreau (*Célestine*), Michel Piccoli (*M. Monteil*), Georges Géret (*Joseph*), Françoise Lugagne (*Mme. Monteil*), Daniel Ivernel (*Captain Mauger*), Jean Ozenne (*M. Rabour*), Gilberte Géniat (*Rose*), Bernard Musson (*the Sacristan*), Jean-Claude Carrière (*the Curé*), Muni (*Marianne*), Claude Jaeger (*the Judge*), Dominique Sauvage (*Claire*), Madeleine Damien, Geymond Vital, Jean Franval, Marcel Rouzé, Jeanne Pérez, Andrée Tainsy, Françoise Bertin, Pierre Collet, Aline Bertrand, Joelle Bernard, Dominique Zardi, Michelle Daquin, Marcel Le Floch, Marc Eyraud, Gabriel Gobin.
Start of shooting: 21 Oct. 1963.
French première: 4 Mar. 1964.

1965: SIMÓN DEL DESIERTO (*Simon of the Desert*) (Mexico). Produced by Gustavo Alatriste. *Dir.:* Luis Buñuel. *Scr.:* Luis Buñuel. *Add. dial.:* Julio Alejandro. *Ph.:* Gabriel Figueroa. *Music:* Raúl Lavista. *Edit.:* Carlos Savage. 42 mins.
CAST: Claudio Brook (*Simón*), Silvia Pinal (*Temptress*), Hortensia Santovana (*Mother*), Jesús Fernández Martínez (*Rabadan, the Dwarf*), Enrique del Castillo (*the Cripple*), Enrique Alvarez Félix (*Brother Matias*), and Luis Aceves Castañeda, Francisco Reigura, Antonio Bravo Sanchez (*Priests*).

1967: BELLE DE JOUR (France/Italy). Produced by Paris Films/Five Films, Rome (Robert and Raymond Hakim). *Dir.:* Luis Buñuel. *Ass. dirs.:* Pierre Lary, Jacques Fraenkel. *Scr.:* Luis Buñuel, Jean-Claude Carrière, from the novel by Joseph Kessel. *Ph.:* Sacha

Vierny (Eastmancolor). *Art dir.:* Robert Clavel. *Sound:* René Longuet. *Music:* none. *Edit.:* Walter Spohr. 100 mins.
CAST: Catherine Deneuve (*Séverine Sérizy*), Jean Sorel (*Pierre Sérizy*), Michel Piccoli (*Henri Husson*), Geneviève Page (*Madame Anaïs*), Francisco Rabal (*Hippolyte*), Pierre Clémenti (*Marcel*), Georges Marchal (*the Duke*), Françoise Fabian (*Charlotte*), Maria Latour (*Mathilde*), Francis Blanche (*M. Adolphe*), François Maistre (*the Professor*), Bernard Fresson (*the Pock-Marked Man*), Macha Méril (*Renée Févret*), Muni (*Pallas*), Dominique Dandrieux (*Catherine*), Brigitte Parmentier (*Séverine, as a Child*), Michel Charrel (*Footman*), D. de Roseville (*Coachman*), Iska Khan (*Asiatic Client*), Marcel Charvey (*Prof. Henri*), Adélaide Blasquez (*Maid*), Marc Eyrand (*Bartender*), Pierre Marcay (*Doctor*), Bernard Musson (*Butler*), Claude Cerval.
Start of shooting: 10 Oct. 1966.
French première: 24 May 1967.

1969: LA VOIE LACTÉE/LA VIA LATTEA (*The Milky Way*) (France/Italy). Produced by Greenwich Film Productions, Paris/Medusa, Rome (Serge Silberman). *Dir.:* Luis Buñuel. *Ass. dirs.:* Pierre Lary, Patrick Saglio. *Scr.:* Luis Buñuel, Jean-Claude Carrière. *Ph.:* Christian Matras (Eastmancolor). *Art dir.:* Pierre Guffroy. *Sound:* Jacques Gallois. *Music:* Luis Buñuel. *Edit.:* Louisette Hautecoeur. 102 mins. (G.B./U.S.: 98 mins.).
CAST: Laurent Terzieff (*Jean*), Paul Frankeur (*Pierre*), Delphine Seyrig (*the Prostitute*), Edith Scob (*the Virgin*), Bernard Verley (*Jesus*), Georges Marchal (*the Jesuit*), Jean Piat (*the Jansenist*), Jean-Claude Carrière (*Priscillian*), Julien Guiomar (*Spanish Priest*), Marcel Pérès (*the Posadero*), Michel Piccoli (*the Marquis*), Alain Cuny (*Man with the Cape*), Pierre Clémenti (*the Devil*), Michel Etcheverry (*the Inquisitor*), Julien Bertheau (*M. Richard*), François Maistre (*French Priest*), Claudio Brook (*Bishop*), Claude Cerval (*Brigadier*), Denis Manuel (*Rodolphe*), Daniel Pilon (*Fran-

çois), Ellen Bahl (*Mme. Garnier*), Augusta Carrière (*Sister Françoise*), Agnès Capri (*Teacher*), Muni (*Mother Superior*), Jean-Daniel Ehrmann (*Condemned Man*), Pierre Lary (*the Young Monk*), Bernard Musson (*Innkeeper*), Michel Dacquin (*M. Garnier*), Gabriel Gobin (*Father*), Pierre Maguélon (*Civil Guard Corporal*), Marius Laurey (*Second Blind Man*), Jean Clarieux (*Apostle Peter*), Christian Van Cau (*Apostle Andrew*), Claudine Berg (*Mother*), Christine Simon (*Thérèse*).
Start of shooting: 26 Aug. 1968.
French première: 15 Mar. 1969; *Italian première:* Feb./Mar. 1969.

1970: TRISTANA (Spain/Italy/France). Produced by Epoca Film, Talía Film, Madrid/Selenia Cinematografica, Rome/Les Films Corona, Paris. *Dir.:* Luis Buñuel. *Ass. dirs.:* José Puyol, Pierre Lary. *Scr.:* Luis Buñuel, Julio Alejandro, based on the novel by Benito Pérez Galdós. *Ph.:* José F. Aguayo (Eastmancolor). *Art dir.:* Enrique Alarcón. *Sound:* José Nogueira. *Music:* none. *Edit.:* Pedro del Rey. 105 mins. (G.B.: 98 mins.).
CAST: Catherine Deneuve (*Tristana*), Fernando Rey (*Don Lope*), Franco Nero (*Horacio*), Lola Gaos (*Saturna*), Antonio Casas (*Don Cosme*), Jesús Fernández (*Saturno*), Vicente Soler (*Don Ambrosio*), José Calvo (*Bellringer*), Fernando Cabrian (*Dr. Miquis*), Cándida Losada (*Bourgeois*), Maria Paz Pondal (*Girl*), Juan José Menéndez (*Don Cándido*), Sergio Mendizábal (*Professor*), Antonio Ferrándis, José Maria Caffarel, Joaquim Pamplona.
Start of shooting: Oct. 1969.
Spanish première: March, 1970; *Italian première:* Autumn, 1970; *French première:* 29 Apr. 1970.

1972: LE CHARME DISCRET DE LA BOURGEOISIE (France). Produced by Greenwich Prods. (Ully Pickard). *Dir.:* Luis Buñuel. *Ass. dir.:* Pierre Lary. *Scr.:* Luis Buñuel, Jean-Claude Carrière. *Ph.:* Edmond Richard (Eastmancolor). *Art dir.:* Pierre Guffroy. *Sound:* Guy Villette. *Edit.:* Hélène Plemiannikov. 105 mins.

CAST: Fernando Rey (*Ambassador*), Delphine Seyrig (*Simone Thévenot*), Stéphane Audran (*Alice Sénéchal*), Jean-Pierre Cassel (*Sénéchal*), Paul Frankeur (*Thévenot*), Claude Piéplu (*Colonel*), Bulle Ogier (*Florence*), Julien Bertheau (*Bishop*), Michel Piccoli (*Minister*), Muni (*Peasant*), Milena Vikotucić.
Start of shooting: 23 May 1972.
French première: 15 Sep. 1972.

E. Unrealised directorial projects

1928: *El Mundo por diez centimos* (scr.: Ramón Gomez de la Serna).

1933: *Les Hauts de Hurlevent* (scr.: Buñuel, Pierre Unik, Georges Sadoul, from Emily Brontë's novel "Wuthering Heights"; NB. Buñuel finally realised this as *Abismos de pasión*, 1954).

1938: various projects at Hollywood on wartime Spain.

1944: *The Sewer of Los Angeles* (with Man Ray).

1946: *The Beast with Five Fingers* (finally filmed by Robert Florey, 1947).

1946: *Ilegible, hijo de flauta* (with Juan Larrea).

1946: *La Casa de Bernarda* (from Federico García Lorcas' play "La Casa de Bernarda Alba").

1950: *Los Amores de Goya*.

1957: *La Femme et le pantin* (from Pierre Louys's novel; finally filmed by Julien Duvivier, 1959).

1957: *Thérèse Etienne* (from John Knittel's novel).

1957: *Los Náufragos de la calle de la Providencia* (NB. Buñuel finally realised this as *El Ángel exterminador*, 1962).

1959: *Beau Clown* (from Berthe Grimault's novel).

1960: *Los Seres queridos* (scr.: Buñuel, Hugo Butler, from Evelyn Waugh's novel "The Loved One"; with Alec Guinness; finally filmed by Tony Richardson as *The Loved One*, 1965).

1963: *Tristana* (scr.: Buñuel, Julio Alejandro, from Pérez Galdós' novella; Buñuel finally realised this, 1970).

1964: *Calandra* (short feature on Holy Week at Calandra; finally filmed by his son, Juan-Luis Buñuel, 1966).

1964: *Quatre mystères* (from "Aura" by Carlos Fuentes, "Las Menades" by Julio Cortazar, "La Gradiva" by Jensen, and "Secuestro" by Buñuel).

1965: *Le Moine/El Fraile* (scr.: Buñuel, Jean-Claude Carrière, from "The Monk" by M. G. Lewis; with Jeanne Moreau; finally filmed, from that script, by Ado Kyrou, 1972).

F. Appearances in films other than his own

1926: *Mauprat* (as extra; dir.: Jean Epstein)
1964: *Llanto por un bandido* (as executor; dir.: Carlos Saura)
1965: *En este pueblo no hay ladrones* (as priest; dir.: Alberto Isaac)

Luis Buñuel on DIARY OF A CHAMBERMAID

Index

(Text only. Filmography excluded)

Abismos de pasión 73
Abysses, Les 144
Acin 40
Adamov, Arthur 142
African Queen, The 72
Age d'or, L' 13, 14ff, 28, 34, 40–41, 58, 60, 62, 66, 68, 76, 79, 91, 94, 100, 106, 109, 120, 126, 127, 130, 132, 143, 155, 156, 164, 174, 177
Alain 95
A las cinco de la tarde 118
Alatriste, Gustavo 117, 118, 127
Alberti 40
Alcoriza, Luis 42, 55, 127
Alejandro, Julio 117
Alphonso XIII, King 35
American Engineering Corps 41
Amour fou, L' 30
Angel exterminador, El 79, 81, 127–137, 138, 145
Angel Guerra 175
Angélus, L' 131
A propos de Nice 13, 14ff
Aranda, J. Francisco 37, 51, 136–137
Arcibaldo de la Cruz 76–80
Arts 140
Aura 137
Aussi longue absence, Une 119
Azaña, Manuel 36

Baby, Yvonne 46, 126
Bachelard 59
Balthus 174
Balzac, Honoré de 88
Bardem, Juan-Antonio 118
Barry, Iris 41
Bataille, Georges 7, 26
Bazin, André 40
Beauvoir, Simone de 28, 119
Belle de jour 131, 165–175, 182
Benayoun, Robert 68
Bergamin, José 40, 128
Bergman, Ingmar 47
Berlanga, Luis 118
Bernanos, Georges 128
¡Bienvenido, Mister Marshall! 118
Blanchot, Maurice 79
Blangis, Duc de 22
Blasetti, Alessandro 55
Blow-Up 165
Borde, Raymond 101, 106, 107
Borowczyk, Walerian 144
Bory, Jean-Louis 140
Bosch, Hieronymus 122
Bosé, Lucia 108
Brecht, Bertolt 53, 142, 143
Bresson, Robert 47, 86, 96, 100

Breton, André 9, 15, 26, 29, 30, 108, 168
Brontë, Emily 109
Brooks, Richard 114
Brunius, Jacques 11, 19
Bruto, El 51, 53–55, 73
Buñuel, Conchita 37
Buñuel, Juan-Luis 90, 130
Buñuel, Leonardo 37

Cahiers du Cinéma 55, 58, 66, 75, 101
Camus, Albert 57, 98
Cannes Film Festival 43, 50, 92, 118, 128, 165
Carmelites 31, 86
Carrière, Jean-Claude 140
Casa de Bernarda Alba, La 42
Casals, Pablo 117
Cela s'appelle l'aurore 62, 91, 102–110
Château de Selliny 22
Chien Andalou, Un 9ff, 15, 40, 109, 120, 134
Chiens perdus sans collier 49
Chute de la Maison Usher, La 110
Claudel 103
Cocteau, Jean 50
Colpi, Henri 119
Combat 140
Communist Manifesto, The 30
Confederacion Nacional del Trabajo 36
Cortazar, Julio 137
Cortes, The 35
Cumbres borrascosas 14, 109, 110

Dali, Salvador 9ff, 28, 40, 109
Dancigers, Oscar 42
Da Vinci, Leonardo 120, 127, 131, 174
Delannoy, Jean 49, 80, 173
Delmas, Jean 74
Delvaux, André 174
Diary of a Chambermaid, The see *Journal d'une femme de chambre, Le*
Diaz, Porfirio 88
Dickens, Charles 88
Divinas Palabras 137
Doniol-Valcroze, Jacques 40
Don Quintín el Amargao 51
Donskoi, Mark 49
Dort, Bernard 142
Dreyer, Carl Th. 47, 110
Duarte, Anselmo 128
Duchamp, Marcel 131, 156
Dutourd, Jean 107

Ekk, Nikolai 49

Él 48, 50, 53, 60–69, 73, 76, 134, 175
Electre 102
Elmer Gantry 114
En este pueblo no hay ladrones 118
En Marge du cinéma français 11
Ensayo de un crimen see *Arcibaldo de la Cruz*
Epstein, Jean 110
Ernst, Max 34, 122, 157
Eros and Civilization 27
Eroticism 26
Eternal Husband, The 137
Etranger, L' 57
Exterminating Angel, The see *Angel Exterminador, El*

Fanny by Gaslight 51
Fellini, Federico 47, 86
Femme et le pantin, La 139
Fièvre monte à El Pao, La 91, 95–102, 105
Figaro, Le 143
Figaro littéraire 140
Figueroa, Gabriel 50, 101, 136
Four Mysteries 137
Francis of Assisi, St. 126
Franco, General 24, 100, 117, 119, 138, 175
Franju, Georges 49, 119
Freud, Sigmund 40, 86, 130–131, 137
Fuentes, Carlos 137

Galdós, Benito Pérez 87–89, 138, 175
Galileo 38
Generale della Rovere, Il 100
Genet, Jean 144
Giono, Jean 139
Giraudoux, Jean 102
Given Word, The 128
Goimard, Jacques 154
Golfos, Los 154
Gómez de la Serna, Roman 40
Goya 122
Gradiva 137
Graham, Billy 47, 87, 160
Gran Calavera, El 42
Gran Casino 42
Grimau, Julian 139
Guillen 40

Handel, G. F. 124, 127
Heaven Knows, Mr. Allyson 72
Hecht, Ben 109
Hija del Engaño, La 51
Hurdes, Las 11, 30ff, 40, 58, 86, 95, 109, 117, 120, 130
Hussard sur le toit, Le 139
Huston, John 72

206

Illegible Son of Flute, The 138
Ilusión viaja en tranvía, La 73, 74-75
Inclan, Valle 137
Isaac, Alberto 139

Jakobson 86
Jensen, Wilhelm 137
Jeune Cinéma 74
Jeunesses Catholiques, Les 23
Jokes and Their Relation to the Unconscious 130
Journal d'une femme de chambre, Le 139-151, 175

Kawalerowicz, Jerzy 119
Kessel, Joseph 168
Knittel, John 44, 139
Kyrou, Ado 14, 55

Lamarque, Libertad 42
Larrea, Juan 138
Last Supper, The 120, 122, 127, 131, 174
Lautréamont 59, 164
Legoshin 49
Lenin 158
Lewis, M. K. 139
Ligue Antijuive 23, 143
Ligue des Patriotes 23, 143
Lincoln Center 29
Llanto por un bandido 139
Lolita 115
Lorca, Federico Garcia 40, 42
Louys, Pierre 115
Lys, Lya 19ff, 62, 156, 177
Mabille, Pierre 69
Maenads, The 137
Magritte, René 10, 157, 174
Maids, The 144
Ma Nuit chez Maud 108
Marcuse, Herbert 27
Marquina, Luis 51
Marx, Karl 30, 86, 158
Mauclaire, M. 23
Maupassant, Guy de 144
Mauriac, Claude 107, 140
Mauriac, François 68
Mers-el-Kébir 41
Messiah, The 124, 127
Michel, Manuel 29
Millet, Jean-François 131, 174
Mirbeau, Octave 139, 140, 142, 148, 149
Moby Dick 72
Modot, Gaston 16ff, 60-62, 68, 76, 91
Monk, The 139
Morazé, Monique 175
Moreau, Jeanne 140
Mort en ce jardin, La 72, 81-87, 91, 112

Most Dangerous Game, The 171
Mother Joan of the Angels 119
Mozart, W. A. 127
Munoz-Fontan, José 118-119

Náufragos, Los 127
Nazarin 66, 87-94, 101, 117, 128, 131, 138, 142, 155, 175
Negrete, Jorge 42
Noailles, Vicomte de 40
Nouvel Observateur, Le 68
Noyau de la Comète, Le 26

Office Catholique International du Cinéma 91
Olvidados, Los 42, 43, 48ff, 55, 139
120 Days of Sodom, The 22
Ortega y Gasset, José 40
Osservatore Romano, L' 119

Papatakis, Nico 144
Paramount 41
Pasolini, Pier Paolo 86, 96
Paulhan, Jean 120
Paz, Octavio 7
Péret, Benjamin 26, 27, 58, 131, 157
Perosi, Lorenzo 38
Persona 47
Petrov 53
Peuple, Le 120
Philosophie dans la boudoir, La 66
Picasso, Pablo 59, 80, 117, 157
Poétique de la rêverie, La 59
Pope John XXIII 126
Portolès, Maria 37
Prévert, Jacques 50, 55, 157
Prévert, Pierre 16, 55
Privilege 114
Provost de Launay, Le 23
Psychopathology of Everyday Life 40

400 Coups, Les 49
Quattro passi fra le nuvole 55

Règle du jeu, La 144
Renoir, Jean 143, 149
Requiem (Mozart) 137
Révolution Surréaliste, La 9
Rey, Fernando 177
Rimbaud, Paul 40
Río y la muerte, El 74-75
Robinsón Crusoe 50, 71-73, 110
Robles, Emmanuel 102
Rohmer, Eric 108
Roots of Heaven, The 72
Rosalie 144
Rossellini, Roberto 47, 86, 100

Ruiz, Raúl 53

Sade, Marquis de 22, 66, 73, 160
Sartre, Jean-Paul 68, 119
Saura, Carlos 118, 139
Schubert, Franz 36
Seguin, Louis 142
Segura, Cardinal 35
Señora Carrar's Rifles 142
Simón del desierto 79, 92, 117, 151-156
Sonatas 118
Song of Happiness 49
Spanish Civil War 41
St. Joan of the Stockyards 142
Storm, The 53
Studio 28 Cinema 23, 143
Subida al cielo 50, 55-59
Sueros, Jesus 119
Suisse, La 120
Surrealist Manifesto 24
Susana 51, 53-54

Théâtre du Vieux-Colombier 13
Thérèse de Lisieux 69
Thérèse Etienne 44, 45, 139
Three Sad Tigers 53
Tolstoy, Count Leo 88
Tristana 80, 87, 117, 138, 139, 147, 164, 175-185
Tristan and Isolde 19
Trouille, Clovis 174
Truffaut, François 49
Tual, Denise 42

Unik, Pierre 109
Urgoiti, Ricardo 41

Vampyr 110
Vauthier, Jean 144
Venice Film Festival 165
Vigo, Jean 13
Viridiana 92, 117-127, 131, 142, 175, 177
Vitelloni, I 139
Voie lactée, La 92, 93, 156-164, 175
Voyage surprise 55

Wagner, Richard 109
Warner Bros 41
Watkins, Peter 114
Way to Life, The 49
Wuthering Heights 109
Wyler, William 109

Young One, The 111-115

Zamora, Alcala 36
Zola, Emile 88

207